William Torrey Harris

The Spiritual Sense of Dante's Divian Commedia

William Torrey Harris

The Spiritual Sense of Dante's Divian Commedia

ISBN/EAN: 9783337337407

Printed in Europe, USA, Canada, Australia, Japan

Cover: Foto ©Thomas Meinert / pixelio.de

More available books at **www.hansebooks.com**

THE SPIRITUAL SENSE OF DANTE'S DIVINA COMMEDIA

BY

W. T. HARRIS

BOSTON AND NEW YORK
HOUGHTON, MIFFLIN AND COMPANY
The Riverside Press, Cambridge
1899

TO

MRS. BEVERLY ALLEN

OF ST. LOUIS, MISSOURI

IN MEMORY OF

THE HOSPITABLE ENTERTAINMENT AND ENCOURAGEMENT

THAT SHE EXTENDED TO THE ST. LOUIS ART SOCIETY

AND TO KINDRED ENTERPRISES

IN THE YEARS WHEN THESE STUDIES BEGAN

THIS BOOK IS GRATEFULLY INSCRIBED

BY THE AUTHOR

PREFACE

To this essay on the spiritual significance of the "Divina Commedia" I prefix a few words, interesting only to the few who study works of literature for spiritual insight. Such insight is of very slow growth, and though I cannot be permitted to claim anything more than a very feeble approach to it in the reflections which I bring forward here, yet I know that the theme dignifies the writer, and that the circumstances of a struggle to attain a high object are worthy of mention, even if the success of the struggle is not great.

My first reading in Dante began as early as 1858, and continued at intervals for four years, by which time I had completed only the "Inferno," studying it superficially in the original, and using Carlyle's translation as a sort of dictionary and general guide to its meaning, perhaps better described in college slang as a "pony" or "crib." I read also the translations of Wright and Cary of the "Purgatorio" and "Paradiso" at this time.

The poem had attractive poetic passages for me at the time, but as a vision of the future state of any portion of mankind I could not accept it. Its horrors repelled me. After this I began to look for some point of view whence I could see a permanent truth in the poem. The possibility of an inner meaning that would reconcile me to the outer form of a work of art I had already learned in 1861 by studying landscape-painting, and afterward by a like study of Beethoven's masterpieces, and, more especially, of Schumann's "Pilgrimage of the Rose" and Mendelssohn's "Song of Praise."

The "Last Judgment," by Michel Angelo, I had begun to study as early as 1863 in an outline engraving, and by 1865 a permanent meaning had begun to dawn upon me. I saw that the picture presented symbolically the present condition of the saints and sinners, not as they seem to themselves and others, but as they are in very truth. It placed them under the form of eternity, to use the expressive phrase of Spinoza, "*sub specie æternitatis.*" At once Dante's "Inferno" also became clear, as having substantially the same meaning. I saw that the great sculptor and painter had derived his ideas from the poet. The ideas of Thomas Carlyle, in his chapter on "Natural Supernaturalism" in the "Sartor Resartus," seemed to me to offer a parallel thought to the "Last Judgment." Remove the illusion of time, and thus bring together the deed and its consequence, and you see it under the form of eternity. So, too, paint the deed with colors derived from all its consequences, and you will picture its final or ultimate judgment. This interpretation I wrote out in 1868 and read to a circle of friends, sometimes called "The St. Louis Art Society," and it was published in the April number of the "Journal of Speculative Philosophy" for 1869, under the title, "Michel Angelo's Last Judgment." I quote below the passage in which I connected the views of the sculptor and the poet.

It was about this time (1869) that it occurred to me that there is a threefold view of human deeds. First, there is the evil deed taken with the total compass of its effects and consequences: this is the picture of the "Inferno."

Secondly, there is the evil deed seen in its secondary effects by way of reaction on the doer, — a process of gradual revelation to the doer that his deed is not salutary either for himself or for others. The evil-doer at first does not see that his being is so closely connected with the being of society that if he does injury to his fellows, thinking to derive selfish benefit at the expense of others, he always works evil to himself sooner or later. He thinks that his cunning is sufficient to secure the good to himself, and at the same time to avoid the reaction of evil on himself. But the real process of reaction which comes with time teaches him the lesson of the impossibility of divorcing the individual doer from the consequences of his deeds. This secondary process of reaction is a purifying process in so far as it teaches this lesson to the evil-doer. He cannot escape purification to the extent that he becomes enlightened by the wisdom of this experience.

If he sees that he has to receive the consequences of his deeds, he must needs acquire the habit of considering the ultimate effects of actions; he will renounce deeds that can end only in pain and repression of normal growth. Hence a third aspect of human deeds becomes manifest,— the purified action which emits only such deeds as build up the social whole affirmatively, and consequently return upon the doer to bless him continually. The purified human will dwells in the "Paradiso," while during the process of purification it is in the "Purgatorio." It is in Purgatory so long as it is in the state of being surprised by the discovery that its selfish deeds invariably bring their punishment upon the doer, and so long as the individual still hesitates to renounce utterly and entirely the selfish deed. This renunciation, of course, takes place when the soul has thoroughly accustomed itself to seeing the selfish deed and its consequences in one unity; then its loveliness has entirely departed. The taste of a poison may be sweet to the mouth of a child, but it soon produces painful gripes. The child learns to associate the sweet taste and the gripes with the mental picture of the poison, and now the very sight of it becomes loathsome. When temptation is no longer possible, the child is purified as regards this danger.

From 1870 to 1880 every year brought me seemingly valuable thoughts on some part of Dante's great work. I presented these views in lectures to audiences from time to time. In the summer and fall of 1883 I made new studies on the whole poem, and gave a course of ten lectures to a St. Louis audience in 1884 (January to March). The present paper, which was written in 1886 for the Concord School of Philosophy, is a summary of the St. Louis course, with marginal notes added at this time.

In 1886 I came into possession of a copy of Scartazzini's essay, "Ueber die Congruenz der Sünden in Dante's Hölle,"[1] and discovered that many of the conjectures as to the relation between sins and punishments in the "Inferno" which I had set forward in these lectures were already the property of the Dante public through that distinguished scholar's paper in the Annual of the

[1] For a translation of this essay, see *Journal of Speculative Philosophy*, vol. xxii. pp. 21–83.

German Dante Society ("Jahrb. d. deutschen Dante Gesellschaft," vol. iv. 1877). In this valuable article Scartazzini frequently quotes with approval the interpretations of Karl Graul, who seems to have suggested many happy explanations of the symbolism.[1] One would wish to see this work of Graul reproduced in English.

Had I met with Graul's work twenty-five years ago, when I first began to see the inner meaning of the poem, I should have adopted it as my guide. Graul's volume bears the imprint of 1843; but Scartazzini's essay did not appear until 1877, or after my views had taken shape.

In matters of interpreting myths and symbols there is so wide a margin for arbitrary exercise of fancy, that it must be regarded as strong evidence of the probable truthfulness of a theory when two entirely independent readers arrive at the same results in detail. At least, I have been much strengthened in my own views, and have gained in respect for my own way of studying the poem on

[1] In the *Harvard University Bulletin*, "Biographical Contributions," No. 7, edited by Justin Winsor, the Dante Collections in Harvard College and Boston Public Library, Part I., by William Coolidge Lane, 1885," I find the work of Graul named under No. 208: "Göttliche Komoedie in's Deutsche uebertragen, und historisch, aesthetisch, und vornehmlich theologisch erläutert von Karl Graul. Leipzig, 1843." Only the *Inferno* published.

reading the thoughts of the greatest of living Dante scholars and finding so many coincidences.

I quote here some passages from my essay on "The Last Judgment" above referred to, published in April, 1869, in the "Journal of Speculative Philosophy:" —

"Michel Angelo passes by all subordinate scenes and seizes at once the supreme moment of all History, — of the very world itself and all that it contains. This is the vastest attempt that the artist can make, and is the same that Dante has ventured in the 'Divina Commedia.'

"In Religion we seize the absolute truth as a process going on in Time: the deeds of humanity are judged 'after the end of the world.' After death Dives goes to torments, and Lazarus to the realm of the blest.

"The immense significance of the Christian idea of Hell as compared with the Hades of Greek and Roman Mythology we cannot dwell upon. This idea has changed the hearts of mankind. That man by will determines his destiny, and that 'between right and wrong doing there is a difference eternally fixed,' — this dogma has tamed the fierce barbarian blood of Europe, and is the producer of what we have of civilization and freedom in the present time. In the so-called heathen civilizations there is a substratum of fate presupposed under all individual character which prevents the complete return of the consequences of individual acts upon their author. Thus the citizen was not made completely universal by the laws of the state as in modern times. The Christian doctrine of Hell is the first appearance in a conceptive form of this deepest of all comprehensions of Personality; and out of it have grown our modern humanitarian doctrines, however paradoxical this may seem.

"In this supreme moment all worldly distinctions fall away, and the naked soul stands before Eternity with naught save the pure essence of its deeds to rely upon. All souls are equal before God so far as mere worldly eminence is concerned. Their inequality rests solely upon the degree that they have realized the Eternal will by their own choice.

"But this dogma, as it is held in the Christian religion, is not merely a dogma; it is the deepest of speculative truths. As such it is seized by Dante and Michel Angelo, and in this universal form every one must recognize it if he would free it from all narrowness and sectarianism. The point of view is this: The whole world is seized at once under the form of Eternity; all things are reduced to their lowest terms. Every deed is seen through the perspective of its own consequences. Hence every human being under the influence of any one of the deadly sins — Anger, Lust, Avarice, Intemperance, Pride, Envy, and Indolence — is being dragged down into the Inferno just as Michel Angelo has depicted. On the other hand, any one who practices the cardinal virtues — Prudence, Justice, Temperance, and Fortitude — is elevating himself toward celestial clearness.

"If any one will study Dante carefully he will find that the punishments of the 'Inferno' are emblematical of the very states of mind one experiences when under the influence of the passions there punished. To find the punishment for any given sin, Dante looks at the state of mind which it causes in the sinner, and gives it its appropriate emblem. The angry and sullen are plunged underneath deep putrid mud, thus corresponding to the state of mind produced by anger. If we try to understand a profound truth, or to get into a spiritual frame of mind when terribly enraged, we shall see ourselves in putrid mud, and breathing its thick, suffocating exhalations. So, too, those who yield to the lusts of the flesh are blown about in thick darkness by violent winds. The avaricious carry heavy weights; the intemperate suffer the eternal rain of foul water, hail, and snow (dropsy, dyspepsia, delirium tremens, gout, apoplexy, etc.).

"So Michel Angelo in this picture has seized things in their essential nature : he has pierced through the shadows of time, and exhibited to us at one view the world of humanity as it is in the sight of God, or as it is in its ultimate analysis. Mortals are there, not as they seem to themselves or to their companions, but as they are when measured by the absolute standard, — the final destiny of the spirit. This must recommend the work to all men of all times, whether one holds to this or that theological creed; for it is the Last Judgment in the sense that it is the ultimate or absolute estimate to be pronounced upon each deed, and the question of the eternal punishment of any individual is not necessarily brought into account. Everlasting punishment is the true state of all who persist in the commission of those sins. The sins are indissolubly bound up in pain. Through all time, anger shall bring with it the 'putrid-mud' condition of the soul; the indulgence of lustful passions, the stormy tempest and spiritual night; intemperance, the pitiless rain of hail and snow and foul water. The wicked sinner — so far forth and so long as he is a sinner, — shall be tormented forever, for we are now and always in Eternity. 'Every one of us,' as Carlyle says, 'is a Ghost. Sweep away the Illusion of Time; glance from the near-moving cause to its far-distant mover; compress the threescore years into three minutes, — are we not spirits that are shaped into a body, into an Appearance, and that fade away again into air and invisibility? We start out of Nothingness, take figure, and are apparitions; 'round us, as 'round the veriest spectre, is Eternity; and to Eternity minutes are as years and æons.'

"Thus by the Divine Purpose of the Universe — by the Absolute — every deed is seen in its true light, in the entire compass of its effects. Just as we strive in our human laws to establish justice by turning back upon the criminal the effects of his deeds, so, in fact, when placed 'under the form of Eternity,' all deeds do return to the doer; and this is the final adjustment, the 'end of all things,' — it is the Last Judgment. And this judgment is now and is always the only actual Fact in the world."

In an essay on Religion and Art, published in the same journal in April, 1876, I brought forward some ideas on the meaning of Purgatory and its significance in literature, pointing out the manner in which Protestant literature has supplemented its religion by restoring the idea of Purgatory.

"This first great Christian poem (Dante's 'Divina Commedia') is regarded by Schelling as the archetype of all Christian poetry. . . . The poem embodies the Catholic view of life, and for this reason is all the more wholesome for study by modern Protestants. The threefold future world — Inferno, Purgatorio, Paradiso — presents us the exhaustive picture of man's relation to his deeds. The Protestant 'hereafter' omits the purgatory, but includes the Inferno and Paradiso. What has become of this missing link in modern Protestant Art? we may inquire, and our inquiry is a pertinent one, for there is no subject connected with the relation of Religion to Art which is so fertile in suggestive insights to the investigator. . . .

"One must reduce life to its lowest terms, and drop away all consideration of its adventitious surroundings. The deeds of man in their threefold aspect are judged in this 'mystic, unfathomable poem.' The great fact of human responsibility is the key-note. Whatever man does he does to himself. If he does violence, he injures himself. If he works righteousness, he creates a paradise for himself.

"Now, a deed has two aspects: First, its immediate relation to the doer. The mental atmosphere in which one does a deed is of first consideration. If a wrong or wicked deed, then is the atmosphere of the criminal close and stifling to the doer. The angry man is rolling about suffocating in putrid mud. The incontinent is driven about by violent winds of passion. Whatever deed a man shall do must be seen in the entire perspective of its effects to exhibit its relation to the doer. The Inferno is filled with those whose acts and habits of life surround them with an atmosphere of torture.

"One does not predict that such punishment of each individual is eternal, but one thing is certain, — that, with the sins there punished, there is such special torture eternally connected. . . .

"Wherever the sin shall be, there shall be connected with it the atmosphere of the Inferno, which is its punishment. The doer of the sinful deed plunges into the Inferno on its commission.

"But Dante wrote the 'Purgatorio,' and in this portrays the secondary effect of sin. The inevitable punishment bound up with sin burns with purifying flames each sinner. The immediate effect of the deed is the Inferno, but the secondary effect is purification. Struggling up the steep side of purgatory under their painful burdens go sinners punished for incontinence, — lust, gluttony, avarice, anger, — and other sins that find their place of punishment also in the Inferno. Each evildoer shall plunge into the Inferno, and shall scorch over the flames of his own deeds until he repents and struggles up the mountain of purgatory.

"In the 'Paradiso' we have doers of those deeds which, being thoroughly positive in their nature, do not come back as punishment upon their authors. The correspondence of sin and punishment is noteworthy. Even our jurisprudence discovers a similar adaptation. If one steals, and deprives his neighbor of property, we manage by our laws to make his deed glide off from society and come back on the criminal, and thus he steals his own freedom and gets a cell in jail. If a murderer takes life, his deed is brought back to him, and he takes his own.

"The depth of Dante's insight discovers to him all human life stripped of its wrappings, and every deed coming straight back upon the doer, inevitably fixing his place in the scale of happiness and misery. It is not so much a 'last judgment' of individual men as it is of deeds in the abstract; for the brave man who sacrifices his life for another dwells in paradise so far as he contemplates his participation in that deed, but writhes in the Inferno in so far as he has allowed himself to slip through some act of incontinence.

"If we return now to our question, What has become of the purgatory in modern literature? a glance will show us that the fundamental idea of Dante's purgatory has formed the chief thought of Protestant, 'humanitarian,' works of art.

"The thought that the sinful and wretched live a life of reaction against the effects of their deeds is the basis of most of our novels. Most notable are the works of Nathaniel Hawthorne in this respect. His whole art is devoted to the portrayal of the purgatorial effects of sin or crime upon its authors. The consciousness of the deed and the consciousness of the verdict of one's fellow-men continually burn at the heart, and with slow, eating fires, consume the shreds of selfishness quite away. In the 'Marble Faun' we have the spectacle of an animal nature betrayed by a sudden impulse into a crime; and the torture of this consciousness gradually purifies and elevates the semi-spiritual being into a refined humanity.

"The use of suffering, even if brought on by sin and error, is the burden of our best class of novels. George Eliot's 'Middlemarch,' 'Adam Bede,' 'Mill on the Floss,' and 'Romola,'— with what intensity these portray the spiritual growth through error and pain!

"Thus, if Protestantism has omitted Purgatory from its Religion, certainly Protestant literature has taken it up and absorbed it entire."

CONTENTS

SECTION	PAGE
1. Introduction	1

I. THE INFERNO

2. Dante turns from Politics to Literature	14
3. In what sense Hell is Eternal	18
4. The Punishment of the Pusillanimous	25
5. Why Infants and Heathen Sages are in the Limbo	26
6. The Punishments of the Incontinent	28
7. The Relation of Sloth to Anger among the Mortal Sins	32
8. What Form of Heresy is a Daughter of Sloth?	34
9. The Punishment of the Violent	36
10. The Daughters of Envy: Ten Species of Fraud	38
11. The Circles of Treachery, the Daughter of Pride	43

II. THE PURGATORIO

12. The Spiritual Sense of Purgatory	46
13. The Entrance to Purgatory	47
14. Church and State	53
15. The Purgatorial Stairs	59
16. The First Terrace: Purification from Pride	61
17. Second Terrace: Purification from Envy	62
18. Third Terrace: Dante's Purification from Anger	64
19. Fourth Terrace: Sloth and its Relation to the other Mortal Sins	66
20. Fifth Terrace: Purification from Avarice	70
21. Sixth Terrace: Purgation of the Intemperate	71

22. Seventh Terrace: Dante's Purification from Lust . . 71
23. The Terrestrial Paradise 72
24. The Spiritual Sense of Lethe 74

III. THE PARADISO

25. The Ascent to Paradise 78
26. The Heaven of the Moon, or the Ritualists . . . 81
27. The Heavens of Imperfect Wills 84
28. The Pusillanimous, the Procrastinators, and the Formalists 85
29. The Heaven of Mercury. The Love of Fame . . 85
30. The Heaven of Venus. Love as Limited to Special Spheres 88
31. The Heaven of the Sun. Theologians . . . 90
32. The Heaven of Mars. True Heroes 93
33. The Heaven of Jupiter. Righteous Kings . . 94
34. The Doctrine of Salvation 95
35. The Heaven of Saturn 106
36. The Heaven of the Fixed Stars 111
37. The Empyrean. The White Rose of Paradise. The Vision of God 115

IV. DANTE'S MYTHOLOGY

38. The Angelic Knowing 118
39. The Poetic Mythus — What it Embodies . . . 123
40. The Sun Myth; its Significance as Physical Description of Mind 125
41. Homer's Mythus of Hades 128
42. Plato's Threefold Future Life in the "Phædo" . . 130
43. Plato's Mythus of Er. The Purgatory . . . 134
44. Virgil's Æneid. Descent of Æneas to Orcus . . 139
45. Metempsychosis *versus* Eternal Punishment in Hell . 144
46. Dante's Mythus of the Formation of the Inferno and the Purgatorial Mount 146
47. Dante's Mythus of the Roman Empire . . . 149

CONTENTS

48. The Minotaur and the Labyrinth in the Light of this Mythus 152
49. Minos as Judge in the Light of this Mythus . . . 155
50. Other Mythologic Figures used by Dante . . . 155
51. The Mythus of Dante's "Purgatorio" 159
52. The Mythus of Dante's "Paradiso" — Gnosticism . 161
53. The Mythus of the "Paradiso" developed in the Doctrine of the Celestial Hierarchies 165
54. The Heretical Tendency in this Mythus . . . 168
55. The Symbol of the Trinity embodies the Highest Philosophic Truth 171

V. SUMMARY

56. The Doctrine of Sin the Central Theme of the Divina Commedia 173

THE SPIRITUAL SENSE OF DANTE'S DIVINA COMMEDIA

§ 1. *Introduction*

THAT a poem should possess a spiritual sense does not seem to the common view to be at all necessary to it. It must have a poetic structure; but does a poetic structure involve a spiritual sense? It is essential that a poem should be built out of tropes and personification. Its real poetic substance, in fact, is an insight into the correspondence that exists between external events and situations on the one hand and internal ideas and movements of the soul on the other. Rhyme and rhythm are less essential than this. The true poet is a creator in a high sense, because he turns hitherto opaque facts into transparent metaphors, or because he endows dead things with souls and thus personifies them. The poet uses material forms, so that there glows a sort of morning redness through them.

There is something symbolic in a poem, but

there is quite as much danger from symbolism and allegory in a work of art as from philosophy. If the poet can think philosophic ideas in a philosophic form, he will be apt to spoil his poem by attempting to introduce them into its texture. An allegory is repellent to the true poetic taste. The music of a verse is spoiled by the evidence of a forced rhyme. So the glad surprise of a newly discovered correspondence between the visible and invisible is unpleasantly suppressed by an intimation that it is a logical consequence of a previously assumed comparison or metaphor. To force a symbol into an allegory necessarily demands the sacrifice of the native individuality of the facts and events which follow in the train of the primary event or situation. They must all wear its livery, whereas fresh poetic insight is fain to turn each one into a new and original revelation of eternal beauty.

Neither philosophy as such nor allegory can be the best feature of a genuine poem. Nevertheless, there are certain great poems which owe their preëminence to the circumstance that they treat themes of such universal significance that they reflect the operation of a supreme principle and its consequences in the affairs of a world, and hence exhibit a philosophy realized, or incarnated, as it were. Their events and situations, too, being universal types, may be interpreted into many series of events within the world-order, and hence stand for so many allegories. Such poems may be said to have a spiritual sense. Homer's "Iliad," and more especially his "Odyssey," include a philosophy and many allegories. Goethe's "Faust" contains likewise a philosophy, and its poetic types are all allegoric, without detriment to their genuine poetic value.

But of all the great world-poems, unquestionably Dante's "Divina Commedia" may be justly claimed to have a spiritual sense, for it possesses a philosophic system and admits of allegorical interpretation. It is *par excellence* the religious poem of the world. And religion, like philosophy, deals directly with a first principle of the universe, while, like poetry, it clothes its universal ideas in the garb of special events and situations, making them types, and hence symbols, of the kind which may become allegories.

Homer, too, shows us the religion of the Greeks, but it is an art-religion, having only the same aim as essential poetry — to turn the natural into a symbol of the spiritual. Dante's theme is the Christian religion, which goes beyond the problem of transfiguring nature and deals with the far deeper problem of the salvation of man. For man, as the summit of nature, transfigures nature at the same time that he attains the divine. The insight into the divine-human nature of the highest principle of the universe, and the consequent necessity of human immortality and possibility of human growth into divine perfection, includes the Greek principle as a subordinate phase.

It is proper, therefore, to study the spiritual sense of the great poem of Dante, and to inquire into its philosophy and its allegory. What is Dante's theory of the world, and what manner of world-order results from it? Not that we should expect that the philosophic thought of a poet would be of a conscious and systematic order; that would not promise us so much. It is rather his deep underlying view of the world, — so deep a conviction that he knows of no other adequate statement for it than the structure of his poem. If an artist does not feel that his work of art utters more completely his thought than some prosaic statement may do it, he is not an artist.

In fact, a poet may introduce a theory of the world into his poem which is not so deep and comprehensive as that implied in the spiritual sense of his poem. This, we shall see, is often true in the case of Dante, — that his poetic vision has glimpses of a higher world-view than is contained in his interpretation of the philosophy of the schoolmen; and his poetic discrimination of the states of the soul under mortal sin is deeper and truer than the ethical scheme which he borrowed from that philosophy.

Moreover, although allegory is the favorite vehicle for religious revelation, and we have in this, the most religious of poems, a predominating tendency toward it, yet his allegory does not cover (or discover) so deep a spiritual sense as the genuine art-structure of his poem reveals.

In the beginning, let us call to mind the fundamental distinction between Christianity and Eastern religions. In the latter the Absolute or Supreme Principle is conceived as utterly without form and void. It is conceived as entirely lacking in particularity, utterly devoid of attributes, properties, qualities, modes, and distinctions of any kind whatever. Such is the Brahm of the Hindoo or the subjective state of Nirvana of the Buddhists. Such is the western reflection of this thought at Alexandria and elsewhere in the doctrines of Gnosticism and Neo-Platonism. Basilides and Valentinus, Proclus and Jamblichus, all hold to an utterly indeterminate, formless first principle. As a result, it follows that they are obliged to resort to arbitrary and fanciful constructions in order to explain the origin of a world of finite creatures.

Quite different is the Christian view of the Absolute. It holds that the Absolute is not formless, but the very essence of all form — pure form, pure self-distinction, or self-consciousness, or reason. For conscious personality is form in the highest sense, because its energy is creative of form ; it is self-distinction, subject and object, and hence in its very essence an activity ; an unconditioned energy, — unconditioned from without but self-conditioned from within. In this great idea, so radically differing from the Oriental thought, Christianity has a twofold support — the intuition of the Jewish prophets and the philosophy of the Greeks.

The survey of the entire realm of thought by Plato and Aristotle has settled the question as to the possibilities of existence. There can be no absolute which is utterly formless. Any absolute whatsoever must be thought of as self-determining, — as a pure self-active energy, of the nature of thinking reason, although in degree more comprehensive than human reason and entirely without its intermittencies and eclipses.

An absolute which is absolute form — and this means self-formative, self-distinguishing, and hence self-particularizing, living, or, what is the same, conscious personal being — is essentially a creator. Moreover, its creation is its own self-revelation, and, according to this, God is essentially a self-revealing God. Hence Christianity is in a very deep sense a " revealed religion," for it is the religion, not of a hidden God who is a formless absolute, but of a God whose essence it is to reveal Himself, and not remain hidden in Himself.

In the first canto of the "Paradiso" Dante reports Beatrice as laying down this doctrine of form: "All things collectively have an order among themselves, and this is form, which makes the universe resemble God."[1]

Christianity has united in its views the Jewish intuition of holy personality with the Greek philosophic conception of absolute Reason. It has not put these ideas together, — so to speak, — but has reached a new idea which includes and transcends them. Moreover, the deepest thought of Roman national life is in like manner subsumed and taken up. While the Greek has theoretically reached this highest principle of essential form and the Hebrew has discovered it through his heart, the Roman has experienced it through his will or volition. He has discovered that the highest form in the universe is pure will. And this again is only a new way of naming pure self-determination, pure reason, or pure personality. It sees the absolute form from the standpoint of the will. According to this, all activity of the will returns to the doer. Whatever man as free will does, he does

[1] Le cose tutte quante Hann' ordine tra loro ; e questo è forma Che l' universo a Dio fa simigliante.

to himself. Here is the root of Dante's "Divine Comedy."

Dante is a Roman, although he has Teutonic blood in his veins. The Roman world-view preponderates in Italy to this day. According to the view of the absolute first principle as Will, each being in acting acts upon itself, and thereby becomes its own fate. It creates its environment. The responsibility of the free agent is infinite. If it acts so as to make for itself an environment of deeds that are in harmony with its freedom, it lives in the "Paradiso." If it acts so as to contradict its nature, it makes for itself the "Inferno." All acts of a free will that do not tend to create an external environment of freedom will, of course, result in limiting the original free will, and in building up around it walls of hostile fate. Fate is only a "maya," or illusion, produced by not recognizing the self-contradiction involved in willing in particular what is contrary to the nature of will in general.

Since the Absolute is free will, it energizes creatively to form a universe of free wills. But it cannot constrain wills to be free. A created being's will is free to contradict its own essence, and to defy the absolute Free Will of God.

Here is the problem which exercised Paul and St. Augustine — and Calvin. What is the mediation between the free will of the Creator and the free will of the creature? There can be no constraint of the free will except through itself. It makes for itself its own fate. But can it relieve itself from its fate also by its own act? Here is the all-important question.

The creature is a part of creation, — each man is only a member of humanity. His will utters deeds that affect for good or ill his fellow-men. He in turn is affected in like manner by the deeds of his fellows. Here is the secret of the method of the return of the deed upon the doer. The individual acts upon his fellow-men, and they react upon him according to the quality of his deeds.

Hence the individual man by his will creates his environment through and by means of society, so that his fate or his freedom is the reflection of what he does to his fellow-men. Only it is not returned upon him by his own might, but by the freedom of his fellow-members of society.

Here is the clue to the question of salvation. The circle of a man's freedom includes not only his own deeds, but also the reaction of society. Inasmuch as the whole of society stands to the individual in the relation of infinite to finite (for he cannot measure its power), the return of his deed to him is the work of a higher power, and his freedom is the work of grace and not the result of his own strength. This is the conception of GRACE as it occurs in the Christian thought of the world. Man is free through grace, and he perfects himself through grace, or indeed suffers evil through grace; for this conception of Grace includes Justice as one of its elements.

Deeds, then, are to be judged by their effect upon society, whether they reinforce the freedom of others or curtail that freedom. Man as individual combines with his fellows, so as to reap the results of the united effort of the whole. The individual thus avails himself of the entire species, and heals his imperfections.

Looking at human life in this way, Dante forms his views of the deeds of men, and slowly constructs the framework of his three worlds and fills them with their people. His classification and gradation of sins in accordance with their effect on society furnishes the structure of the first and second parts of the poem. His insight into the subjective effects of these sins, — both their immediate effect in producing a mental atmosphere in which the individual breathes and lives his spiritual life, and their mediate effect, which comes to the individual after the social whole reacts upon him by reason of his deed, — his insight into these two effects on the individual gives him the poetic material for painting the sufferings of the wicked and the struggles of the penitent.

There is in many respects an excess of philosophic structure in the "Divine Comedy." That there should be three parts to the poem does not suggest itself as a formalism. But that there should be exactly thirty-three cantos in each part, and, adding the introductory canto, exactly one hundred cantos in the whole, seems an excess in this respect. So, too, when we are told that the triple rhyme suggests the Trinity, we find that the suggestion is a vague and trivial one, approaching a vulgar superstition. So, too, the fact that thirty-three years suggests the years of Christ's earthly life. In the second Treatise (chapter i.) of his "Convito" Dante tells us that it is possible to understand a book in four different ways. There is in a poem a literal, an allegorical, a moral, and a mystical sense (*litterale, allegorico, morale, anagogico cioè sovra senso*). The leading of Israel out of Egypt should signify, besides its literal meaning, mystically (anagogically) or spiritually the soul's liberation from sin, — the exodus of the soul, as it were. He says the literal must go first, because you cannot come to the allegorical except through the literal; it is impossible to come to that which is within except through the without. "The allegorical is a truth concealed under a beautiful untruth." The moral sense of a book is its practical wisdom, — what it contains useful for practical guidance (*a utilità di loro*). But in spite of all his ingenuity, we must, I think, confess that Dante's elaborate syntactical analyses of his love poems in the "Vita Nuova," as well as his disquisitions in the "Convito," seem much too artificial, and that they become soon repugnant to us. They seem a sort of trifling in comparison with the grim earnest which the "Divine Comedy" shows. And yet they furnish, after a sort, a key to be kept in hand while we accompany our poet on his journey.

Two things strike us most forcibly after we have begun to penetrate the inner meaning of Dante, — namely, his fertility of genius in inventing external physical symbols for the expression of internal states of the soul, and, secondly, his preternatural psychological ability in discerning the true relation between acts of the will and the traits of character that follow as a result of the subsequent reaction. But our first impression of the poet must be one of horror at the malignancy of a soul who could allow his imagination to dwell on the sufferings of his fellow-men, and permit his pen to describe them with such painstaking minuteness. We see more of a fiend than a man on our first visit to Dante. But even thus early we are struck, in a few instances, with the apt correspondence between the punishments of the "Inferno" and the actual state of mind of the sinner on committing the sin. On a second acquaintance these instances increase, and the conviction gradually arises that Dante has done nothing arbitrary, but all things through a deep sense of justice and truth to what he has actually observed in the world about him. After we have come to this view we soon go further and begin to note the tenderness and divine charity of this world-poet, and finally we are persuaded that we see his loving-kindness in the very instances in which at first we could see only malignant spite or heartless cruelty.

I. THE INFERNO

§ 2. *Dante turns from Politics to Literature*

IN the year 1300, at the age of thirty-five, Dante found himself in the midst of a gloomy wood of terrestrial trials, his city, Florence, hopelessly divided between factions, and Italy itself in the midst of the terrible struggle between the secular and spiritual powers. The growing power of France, jealous of the Holy Roman Empire, wishes to keep Germany out of Italy. The Pope, likewise, feels obliged to find his interest in siding with France, at least temporarily. The Church seems to have no recourse for the safety of its spiritual interests except in grasping at civil power. The Crusades have brought immense wealth to the cities of Italy, which lie on the way between the East and the West. The upstart wealthy families in those cities contest the supremacy of the impoverished families of the old nobility. There is no solution of these evils. Each faction, if suppressed within the city, at once appeals to one of the parties into which Italy is divided. It obtains the aid of the Pope and France on the one hand, or of the Emperor on the other, and, thus aided, regains its power in Florence. Bloody retaliations, confiscations, conflagrations ensue. What can Dante as Prior of a city like Florence do? He banishes the leaders of both factions. But these factions are not isolated, local matters. They are merely symptomatic manifestations of the universal discord, — the two political parties of Christendom, — and cannot be cured by local surgery. France approaches to aid one of the banished parties; and the Pope, to whom Dante turns for aid, betrays his intention to take advantage of internal factions and foreign intervention in order to weaken the power of the Empire in Italy. The Church, having small political power in the way of direct control over large territories, is obliged to retain its influence through the next means, — to wit, money and intrigue. It is evident enough that there is no honorable career left for Dante in his native city. He looks up to the lofty and shining heights of success, — a worthy object for the ambition of a young man of ability, — and sees in his way before him three obstacles. A leopard with spotted hide, white and black spots, — symbolic of the black and white factions of Florence,[1] — impedes his progress,

---

[1] Symbolic of other things, also, as commentators have shown: "Symbolic of worldly pleasure with its fair outside," and the quiet citizen life checkered with its small joys

so that he is minded to go back and give up his worthy ambition to reach the shining heights, but rather to seek safety in the obscurity of private life. But his youth, the hour of the morning, and the sweet season fill him with hope that he shall be able to capture the leopard with his spots, and bring peace and good government to his native city, when, lo! a lion, the symbol of France and French interests,[1] approaches with head erect and furious with hunger. The very air quakes. He

and alternating cares ; symbolic of sensuality ; also of the business of private life. The chief point is that the *gaietta pelle* distracts him from the ascent, and impedes him so that he is often minded to return. The wolf and lion terrify him. But he hopes (*Inferno*, xvi. 106-108) to capture the leopard with his girdle. He thought that he could, with the girdle of his own strength, conquer the factions of Florence, up to the time when he saw that these were backed by the wolf and the lion. Or does the girdle hint at a contemplated entrance of the order of Franciscans in order to overcome his passion for carnal pleasure? If for *la* we read *alla gaietta pelle*, the leopard should be overcome as something hostile and impeding ; if *la*, then it is one of the causes of good hope, — but hope of what ? Certainly not of ascent of the hill ! — But this will be discussed further in another note.

[1] The lion should be ambition or pride, according to commentators, but it is not ambition in general that Dante encountered, but the special instance of it in French interference.

turns away from before the lion, but only to meet a she wolf (the wolf of the capital at Rome, symbolic of that city, and hence suggesting the papal court),[1] full of all cravings in her leanness, grasping for money and political power. Dante cannot ascend on that road to the glorious summit of a successful and honorable life. He turns from politics to literature. Virgil meets him and informs him that he must take another road if he would attain his object. He must try to make himself useful to his age by holding up to it its true image, as world-poet. He must collect and classify all manner of human deeds, and all manner of states of the human soul (antecedent and consequent on those deeds), and paint a vast picture-gallery of characters for the education not only of his native city, nor even of all Italy, but of all Europe and of nations yet unborn.

Accompanied by Virgil, or the genius of literature, he comes to the Inferno and the Purgatory. Accompanied thereafter by the divine science, "First Philosophy," in the person of Beatrice, he

---

[1] So, too, the wolf means avarice, but not avarice in general; it is only the special instance of it that Dante met when he applied to the papal court for aid in suppressing civil war in his native city. Note that the wolf will be chased into hell by the greyhound, so as to no more block the way to the shining heights.

passes the terrestrial and celestial paradises. Although his life seems at first a failure, in that a public career is closed for him, yet it proves in the event a success in a far higher sense, for his service to mankind proves to be more enduring than he had planned. The Celestial Powers have overruled his counsels, led him through Eternal Places, and given him a more important station on the lofty hill whose shoulders were clothed with the rays of the celestial sun.

§ 3. *In what Sense Hell is Eternal*

Over the gate of the Inferno he reads the solemn words: "Through me is the way into the doleful city; through me the way among the people lost. Justice moved my High Maker; Divine Power made me, Wisdom Supreme, and Primal Love. Before me were no things created, but eternal; and eternal I endure. Leave all hope, ye that enter." [1]

The Christian doctrine of Hell and everlasting punishment, at first so repugnant to the principle of divine charity and grace which is the evangel of the highest religion, needs philosophic interpretation in order that we may endure to accompany Dante further. In the first place, we remark that the doctrine of Hell, as opposed to the heathen notion of Hades, expresses the insight into the

[1] John Carlyle's translation, iii. 1–9.

complete freedom of the human will. In the heathen view, there is always a substratum of fate which limits man's freedom and prevents the complete return of his deed upon himself. It is in Christianity that religion, for the first time, conceives man as perfectly responsible, perfectly free, — a spiritual totality. Hence, too, with Christianity there is possible now a doctrine of immortality that has positive significance. Before Christianity, immortality had not been "brought to light," — *i. e.*, no immortality worth having. According to Christianity, man may go forward forever into knowledge and wisdom and mutual brotherly helpfulness in the universe, lifting up others, and himself lifted up by all the influences of an infinite Church, whose spirit is the Holy Spirit and God Himself.

If man can determine himself or choose freely his thoughts and deeds, he can join himself to the social whole, or he can sunder himself from it. He, on the one hand, can mediate himself through all men, placing his personal interest at the most distant part of the universe, and seeking his own good through first serving the interest of all others; or he can seek his selfish interest directly and before that of all others and in preference to theirs. Thus he can make for himself one of two utterly different worlds, — an Inferno or a Paradiso.

We are come to one of these places, as Virgil now informs Dante: "We are come to the place where I told thee thou shouldst see the wretched people who have lost the good of the intellect."[1]

The "good of the intellect" refers to Aristotle's ethical doctrine of the highest good, which is that of the contemplation of God, — the vision of absolute Truth and Goodness. The wicked do not see God revealed in the world of nature and human history. To them, God is only another fiend more potent than the fiends of Hell. They are conquered, but not subdued into obedience. To them, the good seems an external tyrant, oppressing them and inflicting pain on them. This state is Hell. But even Hell is the evidence of Divine love, rightly understood. For it was made not only by "Justice and Divine Power," but also "by Wisdom Supreme and Primal Love." Recall the doctrine already stated in regard to Form. A formless Absolute cannot create real creatures. They cannot participate in his substance, because that which is finite and limited can have no substance if God is without form and distinctions. With the Christian idea, God has distinctions and self-limitations, — pure form. With this idea the finite can participate in the divine substance without annihilation. Were this blessed doctrine not true,

[1] Carlyle, iii. 16-18.

there could be no existence for finite creatures, even in Hell. For, unless the finite can subsist as real and true substance, there can be no free will and no rebellion of the individual against the species. Rebellion against the divine world-order would at once produce annihilation under the heathen doctrine of a formless God. Even imperfection without rebellion would produce annihilation.

But in Dante's Hell there is alienation from God as a free act of the sinners. But God's hand is under the sinner, holding him back from annihilation. Although you rebel against Me, yet you shall not drop out of My hand into the abyss of Nothingness, and My hand shall sustain you and give you participation in the divine substance. My hand shall sustain you, but it will burn you if you sin and so long as you sin, because your freedom is used against itself in the act of sin.

"Before me," says the inscription, "were no things created, but eternal; and eternal I endure." That is to say, with the creation of finite things Hell is created, because substance, actual divine freedom and responsibility, is given to finite things. Hence even their limitations are made to have essential being, and thus Hell is made by the very act of creating. It will exist, too, as long as the finite is created, — that is, eternally.

A doctrine of the ultimate annihilation of the

wicked is a survival of heathenism, — a doctrine compatible only with the doctrine of a formless God. So, too, is the doctrine of the end of probation for the sinners in Hell. Hell signifies the continuance of free will supported by Divine Grace. Let free will cease, and Hell ceases. Let free will cease, and individual immortal being lapses out of spiritual being into mere physical existence, or at least into lower forms of life, and annihilation has taken effect, and the Christian idea of God as pure form, pure personality, at once becomes impossible.

Free will, therefore, necessarily remains to all people in Hell, and so long as Hell itself endures. Hence, also, probation lasts forever. But probation does not mean enforced salvation. That were equally impossible, and itself also the destruction of the Christian idea of God as pure form. Hell is the shadow of man's freedom; salvation is the substance of man's freedom. No sinner can be compelled to repent. He must be converted through his freedom and not against it.

The state of Hell is a state of rebellion against the divine world-order. The individual seeks his selfish good before the good of his fellow-men, and instead of their good. Accordingly, he wills that humanity shall be his enemies. He is in a double state of self-contradiction, — first, within himself he contradicts his own universality or his own reason; secondly, he contradicts his species as living in the world. This contradiction exists for him in the shape of pain and unhappiness, — hellish torment. But this very torment is an evidence of grace. Were he unconscious of his contradiction, he were free from torment. But such freedom from torment would be annihilation of his personality, for personality — let us define it — is individuality which feels its own individuality, and at the same time its participation with all other individuals. All manner of appetite and desire even is the feeling of one's identity with some external or foreign being. Within the depths of one's self he feels that other. So pain is the feeling of the identity of the self with what is not one's particular self. It is the feeling of identity of the little self which we have really become with that larger self which we are potentially but have not as yet become. Hence pain — spiritual pain — is evidence of capacity for growth that is not exercised.

Here we may see the difference between the state of Hell and the state of Purgatory. The sinner is in Hell when he looks upon his own pain, not as produced by his own freedom, but as thrust upon him undeservedly from without. His case is hopeless, because he must continually get more bitter by the contemplation of his own pain and its undeservedness. Could he by any means get an insight into the world-order and see it truly, he would see that his pain all comes from his own act of freedom, — from his opposition to the social whole; then he would welcome his pain as the evidence of his own substantial participation in his race and in the Divine Being. Then at once he would be in Purgatory. All his pain then would become purifying instead of hardening to his soul. He would have arrived at the good of the intellect, or the perception of the divine human nature of God. In Hell the individual looks upon himself as the absolute centre and measure of all things. In Purgatory the individual looks upon society as the centre and measure, and strives to rid himself of his selfishness. He strives to ascend from his little self to his greater self. He struggles against the lusts of the flesh and the pride and envy of his soul. Such lusts and passions now seem to him horrible when they arise within him, and this is the torment of Purgatory.

In Purgatory nothing can happen to the individual that is amiss, for all pain and inconvenience, all the ills of the flesh and of the soul, are made means of purification, means of conquest over selfishness.

It is obvious that to any sinner in Hell there

may come this insight into his relation to his own misery, especially if the missionary spirit in true St. Francis form comes to him and demonstrates its sincerity by its efforts to relieve him of his pain by sharing it, or bearing it vicariously. The eternal occupation of the spirits of the just made perfect is here indicated. They must sustain themselves in their perfection, or attain higher degrees of perfection, by humbly assisting the souls in Hell to see their true condition and thus get into Purgatory.

The characteristic mood of those in Hell is described by Dante in the third canto: "Here sighs, plaints, and deep wailings resounded through the starless air; it made me weep at first. Strange tongues, horrible outcries, words of pain, tones of anger, voices deep and hoarse, and sound of hands among them, made a tumult, which turns itself unceasing in that air forever dyed, as sand when the whirlwind breathes."[1]

§ 4. *The Punishment of the Pusillanimous*

Within the gate of Hell, upon a dark plain, he sees a vast crowd of people running furiously behind a whirling flag, and sorely goaded by wasps and hornets. These are the souls of those who lacked will-power sufficient to decide for them-

[1] Carlyle, iii. 22–30.

selves. They were the pusillanimous who would not undertake anything for themselves, but were the sport of circumstances, external events stinging them to do things and to pursue some aimless giddy flag of a cause. These were not admitted to Hell proper, because they had not developed their free will or power of choice, but yielded to fortune or fate.

§ 5. *Why Infants and Heathen Sages are in the Limbo*

Across the river Acheron we come to "the first circle that girds the abyss. Here there was no plaint that could be heard, except of sighs, which caused the eternal air to tremble. And this arose from the sadness, without torment, of the crowds that were many and great, both of children and of women and men."[1]

These had not sinned, but only failed to enter the Christian faith through the portal of Baptism. Many persons, indeed, had been taken out of this circle and carried to heaven by a "Crowned Mighty One," and we see therefore the limitation implied to the words over the gate: "Leave all hope, ye who enter." Here are left, however, the noble heathen souls and the souls of unbaptized infants. We ask ourselves, What is the meaning

[1] Carlyle, iv. 24–30.

INFANTS AND SAGES IN THE LIMBO 27

of all this? Dante weighed carefully the state of mind of the Greeks and Romans as heathen. With all their enlightenment, they had yet failed to see the world of humanity as divine-human, and with a future like that portrayed in the "Paradiso." For them, there was no Paradiso yet revealed, and hence no Purgatory or transition to it.

Dante truly paints for us the actual world-view as it stood in the Greek mind. It was neither sad nor joyful. "We came," he says, "to the foot of a Noble Castle, seven times circled with lofty Walls, defended round by a fair Rivulet. This we passed as solid land. Through seven gates I entered with those sages. We reached a meadow of fresh verdure. On it were people with eyes slow and grave, of great authority in their appearance. They spoke seldom, with mild voices. We retired to one of the sides, into a place open, luminous, and high, so that they could all be seen. There direct, upon the green enamel, were shown to me the great spirits whom I glory within myself in having seen."[1]

Dante's love of the symbolic thus leads to this allegoric description of his university life (at Bologna?), when he came to the study of literature, and passed over its fair rivulet of speech and entered through the seven gates of the *trivium*

[1] Carlyle, iv. 106–120.

(grammar, rhetoric, and dialectic) and *quadrivium* (astronomy, music, arithmetic, and geometry) through the lofty walls of learning. These heathen were not sinful, not to blame for their lack of insight into the Christian view of the world. Indeed, many of them, like Plato and Aristotle, had worked nobly to make the Christian view possible, as Scholasticism, even in Dante's writings, plainly manifests. But the fact remains that they had not fully attained its point of vision. Their state of mind only is indicated here, and not their eternal condition, unless Christianity rejects its doctrine of human freedom. This, too, is the state of mind of the "unbaptized" children. All children, whether baptized or unbaptized, are heathens up to the time when they can appreciate the world-view of Christianity in some shape, — until they can see nature and human history as a revelation of Divine Reason.

§ 6. *The Punishments of the Incontinent*

Within the real hell of rebellious spirits, beyond the court of Minos, we enter first upon the circles — the second to the fifth circles — in which sins of incontinence are punished, — "those who subjugate reason to appetite," as Dante tells us. In the second circle, which is the first of the "Inferno" proper, the lustful are driven through the darkened air, a long streak of them, borne on the blast like a flock of cranes. Their passions darken the intellectual vision and drive them about "hither, thither, up, down,"— tossed on that strife of windy gusts of passion. The punishment is a realistic symbol of the soul filled with lust. It cannot see truth nor do works of righteousness, for its sky is dark with clouds and tempests. The gluttonous are in "the third circle,— that of the eternal, accursed, cold and heavy rain. Its course and quality is never new; large hail, and turbid water, and snow, — it pours down through the darksome air. The ground on which it falls emits a putrid smell. Cerberus, a monster fierce and strange, with three throats, barks dog-like over those that are immersed in it. His eyes are red, his beard gory and black, his belly wide, and clawed his hands. He clutches the spirits — flays and piecemeal rends them. The rain makes them howl like dogs. With one side they screen the other; they often turn themselves, the impious wretches."[1]

This description of the actual state of the intemperate in this life enables us to recognize the punishments which their sin brings on them. We see the diseases of the flesh personified in Cerberus, — dyspepsia, gout, dropsy, delirium tremens, and what not. Intemperance is utterly hostile to the

[1] Carlyle, vi. 7-21.

good of the intellect, or to any sort of good whatever, and it steeps the soul in its turbid waters and drenches it with its chilly snows or racks it with fevers. In the fourth circle we meet the avaricious: —

"As does the surge, there above Charybdis, that breaks itself against the surge wherewith it meets, so have the people here to counter-dance. Here saw I, too, many more than elsewhere, both on the one side and on the other, with loud howlings, rolling weights by force of chest. They smote against each other, and then all turned upon the spot, rolling them back, shouting, 'Why holdest thou?' and 'Why throwest thou away?' Thus they returned through the hideous circle, on either hand, to the opposite point, shouting always in their reproachful measure. Then every one, when he had reached it, turned through his semicircle toward the other joust."[1]

The avaricious and prodigal are devoted entirely to the unspiritual occupation of heaping up pelf, — they roll the weights by force of chest first one way and then another. Think of the human labor given to property as an end merely and not as a means! The struggle to gain property and save it — the absorption of time and attention required — suggested to Dante the exertion required to roll

[1] Carlyle, vii. 22-35.

heavy weights. The wealthy must needs exert constant pressure to hold together their property; upon the slightest relaxation, the forces that act continually for the dissipation of wealth will gain the ascendency and all will go speedily. The avaricious are engaged in resisting those who wish to have their property to spend for the gratification of want. Property can be gained and saved only by continual sacrifice of the appetite for creature comfort both in one's self and in others. But the longing for property in order to gratify desires has the same limiting effect on the soul as the struggle to save wealth for its own sake. In both cases it subordinates spiritual interests to the service of material things. "*Cosi convien che qui la gente riddi.*" It is the struggle of the hoarding propensity with the propensity to outlay for the gratification of present appetites which produces the vortex in which the avaricious and prodigal are punished. Ill-giving and ill-keeping (*mal dare, e mal tener*) has deprived them of the fair world, — the Paradiso. Dante knows well the uses of property, as we shall see by the numerous punishments in the "Inferno" that relate to its abuse. Property or private ownership is one of the two instrumentalities of free will by which man achieves his freedom. In the circle of the violent, therefore, we see squanderers, robbers, and speculators punished; in the circles of fraud are punished simony, bribery, theft, and counterfeiters. There are seven punishments in all devoted to sinners against the sacredness of property rights and uses.

§ 7. *The Relation of Sloth to Anger among the Mortal Sins*

In the fifth circle we come upon the river Styx, and encounter the souls of the wrathful and melancholy.

" We crossed the circle to the other bank, near a spring, that boils and pours down through a cleft which it has formed. The water was darker far than perse. And we, accompanying the dusky waves, entered down by a strange path. This dreary streamlet makes a marsh that is named Styx when it has descended to the foot of the gray malignant shores. And I, who stood intent on looking, saw muddy people in that bog, all naked and with a look of anger. They were smiting each other, not with hands only, but with head and with chest and with feet, maiming one another with their teeth, piece by piece. . . . There are people underneath the water, who sob and make it bubble at the surface, as thy eye may tell thee, whichever way it turns. Fixed in the slime, they say: Sullen were we in the sweet air that is gladdened by the Sun, carrying lazy smoke within our hearts; now lie we sullen here in the black mire. This hymn they gurgle in their throats, for they cannot speak it in full words." [1]

The seven mortal sins should be lust, gluttony, avarice, sloth, anger, envy, and pride. In the "Purgatorio" (where each mortal sin appears as an inner tendency or incitement, but is not allowed to come to external acts or deeds) these seven sins are expressly enumerated and assigned each to its separate circle. But sloth is not assigned to a separate round of the "Inferno," nor indeed is envy or pride. These are punished in what the Scholastic theologians call the daughters of these mortal sins, — that is to say, in their results.

But St. Thomas Aquinas names six daughters to sloth (*accidia* — ἀκήδεια), — malice, rancor, pusillanimity, despair, torpor, and wandering thoughts. Hence slothfulness is punished in its effects in sullenness and rancor, and also in the round of suicides in the circle of the violent, who take their own lives through despair. Moreover, its daughters pusillanimity, torpor, and scatter-brains are not admitted into Hell proper, but are pursuing the aimless, giddy flag around the shores of Acheron. Anger is punished directly in itself, in so far as it is a wrathful state of mind, by the muddy state of the soul which it engenders, and by the

[1] Carlyle, vii. 100–126.

thick, lazy smoke it causes in the heart. The wrathful is thus far removed from the celestial state of the soul, which discerns truth and wills the good.

The daughters of anger are punished in the rounds of violence below, — the violent against God, against self, against one's neighbor.

The spiritual state of the soul under the influence of anger is well symbolized by immersion in the muddy pool, sobbing and bubbling; the comparison of a sullen disposition to a lazy smoke (*accidioso fummo*), which obscures the light of day and disinclines to all acts of duty, is felicitous. Anger is indeed the muddy state of the soul. No insight into truth, or into reasonable practical works, can exist in the angry soul.

§ 8. *What Form of Heresy is a Daughter of Sloth?*

To our surprise we come here, before reaching the circle of violence, upon heretics burned in tombs.

"As at Arles, where the Rhone stagnates, as at Pola near the Quarnaro Gulf, which shuts up Italy and bathes its confines, the sepulchres make all the place uneven, — so did they here on every side, only the manner here was bitterer. For among the tombs were scattered flames, whereby they were made all over so glowing that iron more hot no craft requires. Their covers were all raised up, and out of them proceeded moans so grievous that they seemed indeed the moans of spirits sad and wounded. . . . These are the Archheretics with their followers of every sect; and, much more than thou thinkest, the tombs are laden. Like with like is buried here; and the monuments are more and less hot." [1]

"In this part are entombed with Epicurus all his followers, who make the soul die with the body." [2]

Is heresy a daughter of sloth? It is supposed to be a daughter of the opposite of sloth, — namely, of intellectual violence, — and in that case it belongs to the progeny of anger. But it is not heresy in general that we have here in the sepulchres, but the heresy of disbelief in the immortality of the soul. Perhaps, however, this seemed in Dante's eyes the effect of intellectual sloth. To them who believe that the soul dies with the body, this earth is only one vast tomb in which they are slowly consumed. So long as they live, they sit and feel themselves wasting in tombs with the lids raised. At death the lids are to close forever upon them. Dante accurately depicts the spiritual state of the soul in this life when possessed of the conviction

[1] Carlyle, ix. 112–131.   [2] Ibid., x. 13–15.

that materialism produces. He supposes this to be the doctrine of Epicurus, — namely, that we die with the body. The sin itself is its own punishment. Moreover, even the view that he takes of the world is to the materialist his hell.

A point of interest is found in the discourse of Farinata to the effect that spirits who can foretell particulars of Dante's exile yet do not know the present. Spirits, on separation from their bodies, it would seem, lose the instrument by which they read the processes going on upon the earth. They know the total possibility of all things, but do not know exactly where the present has brought the process of unfolding it. This is the doctrine of the Scholastics (and of Homer as well). After time — *i. e.*, after all possibility is unfolded — the portals of experience are closed (because there is nothing new any more to become event).

§ 9. *The Punishment of the Violent*

The first round of the circle of violence contained murderers, tyrants, and robbers, quite as we should expect to find them, immersed in blood up to their eyebrows.

Next, the gloomy wood of self-murderers, the fruit of desperation chiefly caused by careless use of property. The suicides are pursued by hell-hounds, importunate creditors, no doubt, and the cares and worries that attend on poverty. With striking poetic justice those who slay themselves are placed, not in animal bodies, but in trees. Their punishment is to need their bodies. This also hints at the vegetative state — a sort of paralysis of will and sensibilities, of feeling and locomotion — of the soul which has come under the influence of settled melancholy.

In the third round of violence are punished the violent against God — the blasphemers.

"Over all the great sand, falling slowly, rained dilated flakes of fire, like those of snow in Alps without a wind. As the flames which Alexander, in the hot regions of India, saw fall upon his host, entire to the ground — whereat he with his legions took care to tramp the soil, for the fire was more easily extinguished while alone — so fell the eternal heat, by which the sand was kindled, like tinder beneath the flint and steel, redoubling the pain. Ever restless was the dance of miserable hands, now here now there, shaking off the (flakes) fresh burning."[1]

Fierce arrogance, like that of Capaneus, attacks the divine mediation in the world in so far as it appears as benign influences, and this hostility turns such influences into tormenting flames. This will be fully evident in considering the sin of Pride later on. It is not easy to distinguish the sin of

[1] Carlyle, xiv. 28–42.

Pride from this of violence against God. In fact, Dante makes Virgil speak of the pride of Capaneus (*la tua superbia*) [1] as that which chiefly punishes him.

The souls punished in the outermost verge of the seventh circle [2] are the violent against art; they are usurers and injurious extortioners, or, perhaps, better designated in our day as speculators in the necessaries of life, — those who try to make fortunes by cornering the food and clothing of the market, and not capitalists who put their money to good uses. These usurers are not to be recognized by their faces, but solely by their moneybags and armorial bearings, behind which they are hidden. They sit crouched upon the burning sand quite subordinate to the pelf they are accumulating. They have lost human semblance, or their humanity has shrunk behind their nefarious occupation.

§ 10. *The Daughters of Envy: Ten Species of Fraud*

The daughters of Envy, according to Dante, are ten species of fraud. These sins are punished in "malebolge," or evil ditches.

Horned demons scourge the seducers and panders. The flatterers wallow in filth. They are

[1] *Inferno,* xiv. 64.   [2] xvii. 43–78.

engaged in destroying the rational self-estimate of those that they flatter by calling good evil and evil good, and producing a confusion between clean and unclean. The Simonists buy and sell the gifts of the Church for money, and are plunged, like coin, head first into round holes or purses, while flames scorch the soles of their feet. As others follow them, they sink toward the bottom of the earth, gravitating toward pelf. Their deeds directly destroy the spiritual by making it subservient to money and material gain; they invert the true order of the spiritual and material, and symbolically place the head where the feet should be.

In the fourth ditch come the diviners, soothsayers, astrologers, or fortune-tellers, who make a trade of a knowledge of the future.

"Through the circular valley I saw a people coming, silent and weeping, at the pace which the litanies make in this world. When my sight descended lower on them, each seemed wondrously distorted from the chin to the commencement of the chest, so that the face was turned toward the loins; and they had to come backward, for to look before them was denied. Perhaps by force of palsy some have been thus quite distorted; but I have not seen, nor do I believe it to be so."[1]

Whether the knowledge of the future be real

[1] Carlyle, xx. 7–18.

or only pretended, it is all the same, for the effect of foretelling what will happen in the future is to utterly paralyze the human will. What is fated to happen cannot be helped. He who divines his own future learns to depend on luck and chance and external fortune, and not on his own reason and will. Moreover, the one who knows the future knows it as already happened, and hence turns all events into something that has already happened, — that is to say, into a past. For him there is no present or future; all is past time. Hence the meaning of the punishment by twisting the head around so as to look backward. They look at all as past, instead of standing like rational beings between the past and future, and, on the basis of the accomplished facts of the past, building new possibilities into facts by the exercise of their wills.

In the fifth ditch are punished the sinners who sell public offices for money. They sell justice, too, for money, thus confusing all moral order. They are plunged in boiling pitch, and tormented by demons with long forks. Dante is actually diverted at the punishment of these mischief-makers, with whom he has become so well acquainted through the politics of his time.

The nature of bribes and bartery is likened to pitch, because it never leaves the person free. A bargain is never closed, but gives occasion for an indefinite succession of demands for blackmail afterward, it is of so sticky a character.

The hypocrites are in the sixth circle.

"There beneath we found a painted people, who were going around with steps exceeding slow, weeping, and in their look tired and overcome. They had cloaks on, with deep hoods before their eyes, made in the shape that they make for the monks at Cologne. Outward they are gilded, so that it dazzles; but within all lead, and so heavy that Frederick's compared to them were straw. Oh, weary mantle for eternity!"[1]

This device of gilded cloaks of lead and deep hoods, all so heavy that they who wear them are tired and overcome, is a symbol ready to suggest itself to a poet. These hypocrites assume forms of disguise, — wear assumed characters, not their own natural, spontaneous characters, but they impersonate characters that they wish to seem. This requires special effort, an eternal make-believe, continual artificial effort to do what ought to require no effort. They are punished by their very deeds in this weary manner.

The seventh ditch is full of thieves turning into serpents. Continual metamorphoses are going on, — serpents into men and men into serpents, the

[1] Carlyle, xxiii. 58–67.

thief nature taking possession of the man by fits and starts. Thievery destroys property, and the thieves have their very persons stolen from them, — even their bodies and personal features, — and are obliged to assume others. We have here a symbol of manifold significance, hinting especially at the disguise which the thief assumes in order to perpetrate his crimes.

Evil counselors in the eighth ditch are wrapped in tongues of flame, the symbol of their own evil tongues, causing flames of discord in the world.

In the ninth ditch are the schismatics, those who have divided religious faith being cloven asunder;[1] those who have produced schism in the State are mutilated about the head, to symbolize the place of their injury to society; while the one who foments schism in the family carries his severed head in his hand, — he has severed the head of the family from its limbs.

In the tenth ditch or chasm we have the falsifiers in four classes: The alchemists who make base

[1] Mahomet is regarded by Dante as a perverter of Christian doctrine, and not as a reformer of the religion of his countrymen. It is interesting in this connection to read Sprenger's great work (*Das Leben und die Lehre des Mohammad*, Berlin, 2d ed., 1869 — see vol. i. 70–90), wherein it is shown how Mahomet derived the first impulse of his career from Ebionitic Christians, heretics who preached in Arabia substantially the doctrine of Islam.

metals resemble gold are punished by cutaneous diseases, symbolic of the superficial effects of their alchemy on the base metals. The simulators of persons are mangled by each other, so as to symbolize the violence done to personality by counterfeiting it. Those who have counterfeited the coin, swelling it up to due weight by alloy, are themselves swollen with dropsy, their blood alloyed with water. The liars and false witnesses reek with fever that produces delirium or double consciousness, for "the liar must have a good memory." He must carry a double consciousness, — one, a current of thoughts corresponding to events as they are; and the other current feigning another order of events consistent with the lies he has told, thus creating within himself a sort of delirium.

§ 11. *The Circles of Treachery, the Daughter of Pride*

Envy is distinguished from Pride by the philosophers in a manner somewhat different from Dante's poetic treatment. Even Dante himself, defining as a philosopher, does not quite agree with himself as poet. One would say that Dante as poet conceives pride to indicate absolute selfishness, or rather concentration on self. Pride says, in fact, to the universe: "I do not want you, or any of your good; I want no participation with you!"

While envy wants the good of others, but wishes evil to be given to them in its stead. Thus, envy has some sociality about it, though of a negative sort. It is still interested enough in its fellows to wish them evil and to covet their good. As ordinarily defined, it would be easy to classify most of the instances of pride under envy.

Just as in the case of sloth, anger, and envy, so here pride is represented by its daughters, which are four species of treachery, — treachery toward one's blood relatives in the family, treachery toward one's native country, treachery toward one's friends, and treachery toward one's masters or benefactors. Caina, named from Cain, holds the first; the Antenora (from Antenor, who betrayed Troy to the Greeks) holds the second class; the Ptolemæa, named from the captain of Jericho who betrayed Simon the high-priest, holds the third class: while the Judecca, named from Judas, holds the fourth class, — Judas, Cassius, and Brutus being crunched in the three mouths of the monster traitor, Lucifer.

The entire circle of treachery is covered with ice, to symbolize the isolating and freezing character of the crime of treachery, the daughter of Pride. This sin alone completely isolates each man from every other. All the others attack the social bond, but are inconsistent, because they seek the fruits of society though aiming a blow at its existence. Pride is consistent selfishness, because it makes itself sole end and sole means. It is frozen, and it freezes all others.

The next branch of our subject is the new view of these mortal sins from the inner or subjective standpoint. After repentance begins, there is no more sin uttered in deeds, but there yet remains the pain that comes from the repressed proclivity within. Hence a series of torments belong to the Purgatory, but essentially different from those of the Inferno.

II. THE PURGATORIO

§ 12. *The Spiritual Sense of Purgatory*

THE chief thought that has guided us in our interpretation of the "Inferno" is this: —

Dante describes each punishment in such a manner that we are to see the essential condition produced in the soul by the sin. The sin itself is beheld as punishment, for each sin cuts off in some peculiar manner the individual from participation in the good that flows from society. In the social whole, all help each and each helps all. Each one gives his mite to the treasury of the world, and in return receives the gift of the whole, — he gives a finite and receives an infinite. Now, each one of the seven mortal sins obstructs in some way this participation.

Let us only look upon the mortal sin with wise illumined eyes — with a spiritual sense, as it were — and we see that the sin makes an atmosphere of torment and embarrassment within the soul, and an environment of hatred between the soul and society.

Dante, therefore, has only to look into the state

of the soul under sin and describe by poetic symbols its condition. It is not the remote effects of the seven mortal sins, but their direct immediate presence, that furnishes the punishments of the Inferno. The effects of sinful deeds return to the doer, and pain comes from this, too. But Dante has elaborated in symbolic description the internal state which constitutes the sin as being the state of torment. There are two attitudes of the soul, however, in the presence of sinful thoughts, and we have arrived at the second — at Purgatory.

We must read the "Divina Commedia" with this thought in mind: Punishment is not an extraneous affair that may be inflicted after sin, and on account of it. Such external infliction is not divine punishment. That is of a different sort; the punishment is the sin itself.

§ 13. *The Entrance to Purgatory*

On emerging from the dark and gloomy depths of the Inferno, Dante and his guide again behold the stars.

"Of oriental sapphire that sweet blue
  Which overspread the beautiful serene
Of the pure ether, far as eye could view
  To heaven's first circle, brightened up my mien,
Soon as I left that atmosphere of death
  Which had my heart so saddened with mine eyes:
The beauteous planet which gives love new breath
  With laughing light cheered all the orient skies,

> Dimming the Fishes that her escort made:
> Then, turning to my right, I stood to scan
> The southern pole, and four stars there surveyed, —
> Save the first people, never seen by man.
> Heaven seemed rejoicing in their blazing rays."[1]

The two poets have now come to a realm of hope and growth and morning-redness, on the dawn of Easter Day, — a festival symbolic of the rise of the soul out of the Hell of sensuality. They meet Cato, the guardian of the place, his face illuminated by the holy lights of the four bright stars of the Southern Cross. These symbols of the four cardinal virtues — temperance, justice, prudence, and fortitude — flamed thus in the morning sky of the southern heavens; while the three great stars symbolizing the three celestial virtues — faith, hope, and charity — will be seen later, in the evening sky, as mentioned in the eighth canto. Directed by Cato, they proceed toward the shore of the sea; and after Virgil has washed the tear-stained cheeks of Dante with the purgatorial dews, he girds him with a smooth rush, the symbol of humility under chastisement. Dante had thrown his girdle of self-righteousness [2] into the pit of fraud on his descent.

[1] T. W. Parsons's Translation, i. 15-25.

[2] Carlyle suggests this meaning for the girdle which was thrown to the monster Geryon. He had once thought to catch the leopard with the painted skin by its aid: —

> "E con essa pensai alcuna volta
> Prender la lonza alla pelle dipinta."

An angel appears, piloting swiftly over the waves a bark laden with spirits chanting the psalm of

It must be noted that there is a vast abyss separating the upper hell of incontinence from the lower hell of fraud and treachery, — the hell of natural impulse and desire from the hell of considerate, calculating selfishness, which is conscious of the spiritual bond of society, and deliberately sacrifices it for selfish ends. It is the difference between the special or particular and the universal. Incontinence seeks the particular object of gratification, and simply neglects the social bond that would forbid it. But Envy, with its daughters, the ten species of fraud, does not attack the individual directly, but through and by means of the social bond itself. It uses the social bond as though it were not a means of existence for the social whole, but as though it were a means for the individual to use in seeking his private and exclusive ends. So, too, Pride, with treachery, its daughter, seeks to destroy all four forms of the social bond, directly seeking to put the individual in place of the social whole, and to set aside the social bond entirely. Now, the principle of this nether hell is not an animal or natural one, a yielding to native impulse, but a peculiarly human hell (xi. 25, "Ma perchè frode è dell' uom proprio male"), a hell made by using the social bond against itself (fraud), or by seeking to destroy it utterly (treachery). The girdle (of self-righteousness, as Carlyle interprets it, following the hints of older commentators) might then be taken to signify the principle of Dante's actions, — the aim of life which united or girded up his endeavors while a young man looking to wealth and luxury, creature comforts, — individual happiness, in short. It was the principle of thrift that considers the pleasures which the sins of incontinence seek, to be legitimate ends for the deliverance, "When Israel went out of Egypt, the house of Jacob from a people of strange lan-

pursuit of the soul. The love of sex, of food and drink, of money, of pure individual will (anger is based on this), is the object for which the girdle of thrift unites one's endeavors: it is a selfish aim, and, while it may be ever so legitimate in its use of means for gratification, yet it is, after all, akin to envy, and this mortal sin is attracted to it and hopes to prevail upon it. The girdle of legitimate self-seeking, therefore, attracts Geryon, the monster of hypocrisy and kindred vices. Dante has recently seen the nature of these objects of gratification, and is ready to yield up to Virgil this girdle. Scartazzini, in his commentary (Nota A, *Inf.* xvi. 106), holds that the cord is not a mere symbol, but also a real cord — the cord of the Franciscan order, with which Dante had once (according to old tradition) girded himself in the habit of a novice, thinking to tame the appetites of the flesh (prender la lonza). "The cord has become superfluous since Dante has left behind the circles wherein luxury is punished." This cord is used merely to excite the attention of Geryon; or does it suggest to Geryon the approach of an apostate from the Franciscan order, — one who has discarded his girdle of renunciation, a hypocritical Franciscan, secretly unfaithful to the rules of his order (as suggested by Philalethes in his commentary)? This is certainly better than the interpretation of those who take the girdle as a symbol of fraud, or of some virtue opposed to fraud, unless the leopard signifies Florence, and its spots denote the white and black parties, in which case the girdle may mean fraud in the sense of stratagem, or virtue in the sense of justice, or vigilance, or impartiality, as suggested by commentators. But the leopard suggests guage," celebrating their escape from the bondage of sin.

The first terrace of the steep mountain of Purgatory is devoted to the souls who procrastinated their repentance. Manfred tells them that one who dies in contumacy of the holy church must stay on the plain that surrounds the ascent for a period thirty times as long as the period of his presumption. And Belaqua, who has attained the first terrace, is obliged to wait, as we learn, on the first terrace a duration, equivalent to the time he lost in his earthly life by procrastination. But it seems that the time of delay may be shortened by the prayers of pious people still on the earth.

Here we note a striking contrast between the souls that desire purification and those who peopled the rounds of the Inferno. The spirit of those in Hell is that of bitterness against others. They do not look for help from coöperation. Having attacked society by mortal sin, they find their deeds returned or reflected back upon them as pain and limitation. They curse their fellow-men and do not wish coöperation. But if it has attained the "good of the intellect," which is the recognition

---

Florence and quiet citizen life, and also sensuous pleasure or luxury, and perhaps the factions of Florence also. Gayety and liveliness are emphasized in the beast.

of the principle of grace (or beneficence) as the supreme principle of the universe, and its corollary of human freedom and responsibility, the soul is in Purgatory. It now sees all pain and inconvenience to be angels in disguise, — to be, in fact, the necessary means of purification and progress. This mountain of purification is indeed the steepest ascent in the world, but, as Virgil assures Dante, "the more one mounts, the less it pains him;" and "when it becomes as pleasant and easy to climb as it is to float down stream in a boat," then one has surely arrived at the end of his journey. He has rooted out not only the habits of sinning, but also all the proclivities and tendencies to it, and there is no longer any danger of temptation, because the full light of the intellect enables him to see the true nature of all deeds, and he loves the good and hates the evil quite spontaneously.

The divine charity that prays for others, and seeks their eternal good with missionary zeal, avails to help them up the mountain of purification. As the souls who are detained on the first circle on account of their procrastination long for the time when they may enter upon their purgation, they chant the "Miserere," the Fifty-first Psalm, full of longing for purification: "Wash me thoroughly from mine iniquity, and cleanse me from my sin. For I acknowledge my transgressions."

§ 14. *Church and State*

Dante's poem differs from all other works of art in the fact that he does not limit himself to the development of a single event or a single collision of an individual, but shows us in a threefold series more than half a thousand tragic and epic characters, so foreshortened in the perspective of the divine purpose of his poem as to be seen each at one glance of the eye as we pass on our way. His supreme artistic power in this respect appears in his ability to trace all the essential outlines of a character in the fewest strokes. Examples of this abound throughout the poem. The picture of Sordello, as they met him on the first terrace, on the evening of the first day, is noteworthy, especially because of the fact that it betrays the pride of Dante's character in his loving description of the pride of another: —

> "But yonder, look! one spirit, all alone,
>   By itself stationed, bends toward us his gaze:
> The readiest passage will by him be shown.
>
> "We came up toward it: O proud Lombard soul!
>   How thou didst wait, in thy disdain unstirred,
> And thy majestic eyes didst slowly roll!
>
> "Meanwhile to us it never uttered word,
>   But let us move, just giving us a glance,
> Like as a lion looks in his repose."[1]

[1] Parsons, vi. 58–66.

The apostrophe to Italy that follows describes the civil factions, and is one of the many in which Dante proclaims his doctrine of the necessity of separation of church and state, or say, rather, coördination and independence of the two institutions. Human defect as sin must be adjudged and recompensed differently from human defect as crime. Sin is rebellion against the divine world-order, and cannot be atoned for by a finite measure of punishment, but may be escaped only by complete repentance, complete internal change. Sin is essentially internal, while crime consists essentially in the overt act. Crime must be measured and punished, — measured by itself, and the deed or its symbolic equivalent returned upon the criminal. For one tribunal to take cognizance of both phases of defect is to confuse the standards of religion and civil justice. To treat sin as crime, and teach that it may be measured and condoned by some external fine or penance, destroys the religious consciousness. To treat crime as sin makes every slightest dereliction incur the last penalty of the law, and establishes the code of Draco. For the sinner is a rebel or traitor against God. He attacks his own essence, and, if permitted to carry out his will, would actually destroy his individual being. To return his act upon him is to inflict infinite punishment on him. Hence justice — *i. e.*

a formal return of the deed — cannot save the sinner. But there is *grace*, which forgives the sin upon genuine repentance. The Church must look to the state of the heart, — that is to say, to the disposition of the man. The civil power must look to the deed. If the Church administers the State, it looks too much toward the disposition, and makes too small account of the overt act. In correcting its procedure, and in adapting itself to the needs of civil justice, it soon comes to neglect its divine functions, and to reduce religion to an external ceremonial by degrading the idea of sin to the idea of crime, or external act. These thoughts weighed much upon the mind of Dante, and he often recurs to this theme.

The vale of the princes, to which the three poets come on the close of the first day, is in many respects the most charming scene in the "Divina Commedia," although its intent appears to be the reproof of secular potentates for their hesitation, their procrastination in asserting their divine coordination with the spiritual potentate, and thus bringing to an end the distraction of Italy. This suggestion also occurs in the psalm, "Salve Regina," which the princes intone as they sit on the green turf amid flowers. It calls upon the Mother of Pity to save us poor exiles dwelling in this vale of tears, — exiles also from our rightful thrones.

Moreover, the poem hints at the pathos for Dante, himself an exile, on account of this procrastination of the princes to assume rightful authority, and bring peace to the Italian cities.

> " 'Twixt steep and level went a winding path
> Which led us where the vale-side dies away
> Till less than half its height the margin hath.

> "Gold and fine silver, ceruse, cochineal,
> India's rich wood, heaven's lucid blue serene,
> Or glow that emeralds freshly broke reveal,
> Had all been vanquished by the varied sheen
> Of this bright valley set with shrubs and flowers,
> As less by greater. Nor had Nature there
> Only in painting spent herself, but showers
> Of odors manifold made sweet the air
> With one strange mingling of confused perfume,
> And there new spirits chanting, I descried,
> 'Salve Regina!' seated on the bloom
> And verdure sheltered by the dingle side." [1]

The sun goes down, and here no step can be taken with safety after the darkness comes on. The sun of righteousness shines intermittently on this round of ante-Purgatory, and strictest care must be taken to guard against the temptations that come up from the memories of the old life during the night intervals of the soul.

> " 'T was now the hour that brings to men at sea,
> Who in the morn have bid sweet friends farewell,
> Fond thoughts and longing back with them to be;
> And thrills the pilgrim with a tender spell

[1] Parsons, vii. 70–84.

Of love, if haply, new upon his way,
   He faintly hear a chime from some far bell,
That seems to mourn the dying of the day;
   When I forbore my listening faculty
To mark one spirit uprisen amid the band
   Who joined both palms and lifted them on high
(First having claimed attention with his hand),
   And toward the Orient bent so fixed an eye
As 't were he said, ' My God ! on thee alone
   My longing rests.' Then from his lips there came
' Te lucis ante,' so devout of tone,
   So sweet, my mind was ravished by the same ;
The others next, full sweetly and devout,
   Fixing their gaze on the supernal wheels,
Followed him chanting the whole Psalm throughout.
   Now, reader, to the truth my verse conceals
Make sharp thy vision; subtle is the veil,
   So fine 't were easily passed through unseen."[1]

This hymn for the close of day prays for guardianship during the night of the soul from dreams, phantasms, and from the enemy. Temptation has for it the world-renowned symbol of the Serpent in the Garden of Eden.

" I saw that gentle army, meek and pale,
   Silently gazing upward with a mien
   As of expectancy, and from on high
   Beheld two angels with two swords descend
Which flamed with fire, but, as I could descry,
   They bare no points, being broken at the end.[2]

[1] Parsons, viii. 1-21.

[2] The guardian angels, whose swords of divine justice are blunted with mercy through the death of the Redeemer. — Lombardo, quoted by Scartazzini.

Green robes, in hue more delicate than spring's
   Tender new leaves, they trailed behind and fanned
With gentle beating of their verdant wings.
   One, coming near, just over us took stand;
Down to th' opponent bank the other sped,
   So that the spirits were between them grouped.
Full well could I discern each flaxen head;
   But in their faces mine eyes' virtue drooped,
As 't were confounded by excess and dead.
   'From Mary's bosom they have both come here,'
Sordello said — 'this valley to protect
   Against the serpent that will soon appear.'" [1]

The Compline hymn prayed for protection, and it has been answered. Now the "enemy" appears.

            "Sordello to his side
Drew Virgil, and exclaimed: 'Behold our Foe!'
   And pointed to the thing which he descried;
And where that small vale's barrier sinks most low
   A serpent suddenly was seen to glide,
Such as gave Eve, perchance, the fruit of woe.
   Through flowers and herbage came that evil streak,
To lick its back oft turning round its head,
   As with his tongue a beast his fur doth sleek.
I was not looking, so must leave unsaid
   When first they fluttered, but full well I saw
Both heavenly falcons had their plumage spread.
   Soon as the serpent felt the withering flaw
Of those green wings, it vanished, and they sped
   Up to their posts again with even flight." [2]

Within Purgatory proper we are told that there is no longer any temptation. The serpent appears

[1] Parsons, viii. 22–39.   [2] Ibid., viii. 95–108.

no more after passing beyond the terrace of ante-Purgatory.

§ 15. *The Purgatorial Stairs*

Dante is carried in sleep by Lucia (Divine Grace) to the gate of Purgatory, and on the morning of the second day he sees

> ... " a gate, and leading to it went
> Three steps, and each was of a different hue;
> A guardian sat there keeping the ascent.
> As yet he spake not, and as more and more
> Mine eyes I opened, on the topmost stair
> I saw him sitting, and the look he wore
> Was of such brightness that I could not bear.
> The rays were so reflected from his face
> By a drawn sword that glistened in his hand
> That oft I turned to look in empty space." [1]

> ... " We therefore came and stood
> At the first stair, which was of marble white,
> So clear and burnished that therein I could
> Behold myself, how I appear to sight.
> The second was a rough stone, burnt and black
> Beyond the darkest purple; through its length
> And crosswise it was traversed by a crack.
> The third, whose mass is rested on their strength,
> Appeared to me of porphyry, flaming red,
> Or like blood spouting from a vein." [2]

In the "Summa Theologica" of St. Thomas Aquinas,[3] Penitence, which is the theme of Purga-

---

[1] Parsons, ix. 76–84.
[2] Ibid., ix. 94–102.
[3] iii. 90.

tory, is defined as having three parts, *contrition*, *confession*, and *satisfaction*. Dante places the stair of confession first. It mirrors the individual as he appears. Contrition calcines the soul with humility and renunciation, and makes cross-shaped fissures in it where the human passions and appetites are burnt out. Satisfaction or penance is the third part of penitence, and is defined as, first, alms; second, fasting; and third, prayer. Satisfaction consists, therefore, in the repression of selfishness, and especially in the practical seeking for the good of others. Hence the third step flames red with the color of love.

Two keys, golden and silver, the latter of discernment of the heart and the former of authority to give absolution, are in the hands of Peter, the symbol of the power of the Church. Seven *p*'s are inscribed on the forehead on entering Pugatory; one of these seven mortal sins (*peccata*) is to be purged away on each terrace of the mountain.

In the "Inferno" the seven mortal sins were not all punished directly in their abstract form as passions or appetites, but rather in their fruits; for example, "the daughters of anger, of envy, of pride." Here, however, sin is not permitted to triumph and come to its fruitage; nay, it is not permitted even to fill the desires. It can only appear in the soul as an element of struggle in which the will for holiness is victorious.

In purgation from sin, therefore, the sin appears directly in its proper form, and the soul discerns it in its true character as embarrassment and hindrance to its higher life.

§ 16. *The First Terrace: Purification from Pride*

On the lowest terrace souls are purified from pride. To the soul enlightened by the good of the intellect, selfish pride seems to convert human beings into caryatids or corbels bent to the earth by their loads. The soul that makes itself the centre of the universe and strives to live on that principle, finds on his shoulders the entire weight of the world.

"As, to support a floor or roof by way of corbel, one sometimes sees a figure join the knees to the breast, the which, out of its untruth, causes a true discomfort in who sees it, thus saw I these shaped, when I well gave heed. True is it that they were more and less drawn together, according as they had more or less on their backs; and he who had most endurance in his mien, weeping, seemed to say, 'I can no more.'"[1]

These proud souls, thus bowed down beneath the weight of the universe, chant the Lord's prayer, — the prayer taught as the model of true humility

[1] A. J. Butler's translation, x. 130–139.

in contrast to the prayer of the proud Pharisee. Dante's version of this prayer is not only a wonderful paraphrase, but, at the same time, a high order of commentary on its meaning.

Images of humility are sculptured on the cornice of the wall, where those who are bent with pride have the greatest difficulty in seeing them. Ideals of humility are not easily formed in the soul when it is first resisting its inclinations to pride. It can then see only the effects of pride. Hence on the floor beneath their feet are sculptured the examples of pride brought low. These they can see readily when bowed to the earth. When they have recovered a more erect position, they may see the examples of humility. The souls of this terrace feel the true relation of pride to the good of the intellect. They chant the hymn *Te Deum Laudamus*, recognizing God as infinitely exalted above them, while the proud in the Inferno would not recognize God except by blasphemy and violence. At the holy stairs the poets hear the beatitude sung, " Blessed are the poor in spirit," symbolizing the victory over pride.

§ 17. *Second Terrace: Purification from Envy*

On the next terrace the rock has the livid hue of envy. The souls lean one upon another like blind men. " For in all of them a thread of iron bores the eyelid, and sews it in such wise as is done to a wild falcon because he remains not quiet."[1]

These souls perceive the spiritual effects of envy to be the blinding of the soul to all true and just estimate of their fellow-men. Whereas in the Inferno each envious soul rejoiced in his superior craft and tried to break the social bond by fraud, here they mutually support and are supported, and are conscious of their blindness.

As their sight is taken away, they do not behold sculptures, but hear voices in the air, first reciting examples of generosity, and, next, examples of the dreadful fruits of envy.

On entering the stairway to the next terrace they hear the beatitude directed against envy: "Blessed are the merciful." Blessed are they who are considerate of the welfare of others. In spiritual things the more participation, the more each gives to all, the more all give to each, and the greater is the share of each, because the good that is enjoyed by one's fellows is reflected back from them (*E come specchio l' uno all' altro rende*), so that the individual is blessed by all the spiritual good possessed by the whole of society. Herein is contained the doctrine of "the Good of the Intellect" as regards the sin of envy.

[1] Butler, xiii. 70–72.

§ 18. *Third Terrace: Dante's Purification from Anger*

On the third terrace, within Purgatory proper, takes place the purification from anger. Dante himself has given us examples of anger, as we saw in the Inferno,— for instance, in his treatment of Bocca degli Abati, whose hair he pulled so cruelly. In the round of anger, and still more in the round of treachery, he seemed to give way to anger. He made some effort to justify himself symbolically on the ground that it was his hatred of the sins that made him mistreat the sinners. Even Virgil approves[1] of his rage against Filippo Argenti, formerly an arrogant personage (*persona orgogliosa*), but now weeping (*vedi che son un che piango*). Why should he be spiteful toward some of the sinners in the Inferno and pitiful toward others? His own weaknesses and proclivities are painted by his sympathies and aversions. On this third terrace, however, he seems to confess his own sin, and suffers the pain of purification like the other penitents.

"We were going through the evening, gazing onward, as far as the eyes could reach, against the late and shining rays, and beheld little by little a smoke draw towards us, as the night obscure; nor

[1] *Inferno*, viii. 44, 45.

from that was there place to withdraw one's self; this took from us our eyes and the pure air."[1]

"Gloom of hell, and of a night bereft of every planet under a poor sky, darkened all that it can be by cloud, made not to my sight so thick a veil as that smoke which there covered us, nor of so harsh a texture to feel; for it suffered not the eye to stay open; wherefore my learned and faithful escort moved to my side and offered me his shoulder. Just as a blind man goes behind his guide in order not to stray, and not to stumble against aught that can harm him or maybe slay him, I was going through the bitter and foul air listening to my leader, who said only: 'See that thou be not cut off from me.' I began to hear voices, and each appeared to be praying for peace and mercy to the Lamb of God who takes away sins. Only Agnus Dei were their preludes; one word in all there was, and one measure, so that there appeared among them all concord."[2]

In this terrace, examples of meekness, and of anger its opposite, flash before the mind in visions as they walk onward through the stifling smoke. Dante listens eagerly to another discussion of the separate functions of church and state, and of the bad government in that state where "the shepherd who goes before may chew the cud, but has not

[1] Butler, xv. 139-145.   [2] Ibid., xvi. 1-15.

the hooves divided." The leader ruminates (*i. e.* chews the cud), or theorizes and comes to know divine wisdom as a teacher, but does not discriminate in temporal affairs and divide good from evil conduct (*discretionem boni et mali*, as St. Thomas suggests).

At the close of the second day they reach the stairway, and hear the beatitude directed against anger: " Blessed are the Peacemakers !"

§ 19. *Fourth Terrace: Sloth and its Relation to the other Mortal Sins*

On the fourth terrace Virgil explains to Dante the relation of the seven mortal sins to each other, newly defining them all. Love is the common ground. Love remiss is sloth, the mortal sin purged away on this terrace. Love perverted by selfishness becomes love of evil to one's neighbor, and forms the essence of the three sins, — pride, envy, and anger. Love excessive is the basis of the three sins of incontinence, — lust, gluttony, and avarice.

These sins are called mortal or deadly because they attack the conditions of spiritual life, or, what is the same thing, the foundations of the institutions of civilization. Pride, the most deadly of the seven, strikes not only against the fruits of social union, but also against the essence of social union in itself. It refuses to associate. Its aim is to isolate itself from the universe. Hence its fruits are treachery in the family, the state, and the church. It aims blows directly against the existence of the social bond. Its effect on the soul is symbolized by the frozen lake Cocytus.

Envy is not so deadly as pride, but far more fatal than anger. Envy, by means of fraud, strikes against the social tie that binds society together; while anger induces violence, which strikes only particular individuals and not the social bond. Envy strikes against the institution of property, rendering it insecure, and destroying the trust of men in the means of achieving their freedom from wants of food, clothing, and shelter. It attacks personality itself by hypocrisy, flattery, fraudulent impersonation, evil counsel, and schism, rendering every man distrustful of his fellows. But it does not isolate man so deeply and in so deadly a manner as Pride. Pride severs all social intercourse; while Envy desires to reap the fruits of social life, but at the expense of society itself, thus setting up a contradiction in the form of its effort. Envy wishes to appropriate the good of men, but through their loss; Pride wishes no share either in society or in its fruits.

Anger produces these evils in a less degree, because it is special in the character of its effects.

Avarice and Waste injure society by diverting property from its place as a means of realizing human freedom. The social interchange by which the individual is enabled to contribute something of his own deeds for the benefit of his fellow-men, and to draw out in his turn from the market of the world his share in its aggregate of productions, is rendered possible by means of the institution of private property. There could be no transfer of the individual will to the social whole unless the individual could impress his will on things and make them his property. Consequently, without the institution of private property, he could not help society, and this would render impossible, on the other hand, his participation in the labor of the race, — he could receive nothing from his fellow-men, because nothing could be collected or transmitted. Hence the significance of property, and hence the deadliness of the sin which perverts property from its usefulness by avarice or wastefulness.

Gluttony is more of a private nature than avarice. Avarice touches at once the material bond of the practical will-power of society; while gluttony or intemperance unfits the individual to fulfill his functions as a member of institutions, the family, civil society, the state, the church. Consequently the good that would flow from him is greatly diminished or entirely cut off. He sinks down below the condition of a brute and follows appetite alone, thus paralyzing his will, and cutting himself off from the dominion over nature in time and space.

Lust attacks the institution of the family. It is a deadly sin, because the family is the element of all other institutions, their material presupposition. It is placed above intemperance, because the latter is nearly as destructive to the family, and directly more destructive to the industrial well-being of society, and because intemperance leads more directly to the sins of sloth and anger. Each nation has its besetting sins. Our Norman Anglo-Saxon race, most given to independent individuality of all races, is, perhaps, liable to pride and avarice more than other nations, showing its individuality against the state, and using its free will in creating an independence in the shape of a private fortune; and, on the other hand, it is perhaps more inclined than other peoples to respect the sacredness of the family. Hence lust would change places with avarice or pride in the hierarchy of sins, as formulated by a theologian of Old or New England.

After the new definition of the mortal sins and their reduction to a system by Virgil, he proceeds in the eighteenth canto to discourse on ethics. The hour of midnight has approached, and the poets, seated at the top of the stairway, are looking at the gibbous moon in the west, when suddenly they are startled by a mighty rout of souls, who are purging away the sin of sloth by running furiously and shouting instances of zeal and energy. This example of zeal is all the more surprising after the words of Sordello relative to the effect of darkness on the soul in ante-Purgatory: "To go upward in the night is not possible; even this line thou couldst not pass after the set of sun." We note here that the moon, or the reflected light of mere forms and ceremonies, serves to guide the reformed slothful people.

Later in the night Dante dreams the dream of the Siren who (symbol of the sin here purged away) charms one aside from the labors of duty, and plunges him in a dream of slothful ease and luxury. It is remarked that sloth assails the whole range of moral virtues, theoretical and practical.

§ 20. *Fifth Terrace: Purification from Avarice*

On the fifth terrace Dante sees the purification from avarice, people realizing its groveling nature as taking the mind off from spiritual things and placing them on things of earth earthy. In Canto xx. we hear a brief *résumé* of French history, — hinting of the relation of the French nation to avarice (its bribery by the papal court). The mountain trembles, and the hymn "Gloria in Excelsis" peals out, and the shade of the poet Statius emerges from the terrace below into the fifth. All souls in a state of penitence rejoice and praise God when one of their number makes progress.

§ 21. *Sixth Terrace: Purgation of the Intemperate*

On the sixth terrace the intemperate resist their inordinate appetites in the presence of food and drink that invite the senses. To them, gluttony is a fetter fastening the spirit to food and drink so that it is not able to attend to spiritual matters. Instead of eating and drinking with their mouths, they recall the words of the Psalmist: "Open thou my lips, and my mouth shall show forth thy praise." They will to hunger and thirst after righteousness, and not after other food.

§ 22. *Seventh Terrace: Dante's Purification from Lust*

On the seventh terrace the sin of lust is purged by fire. The souls realize that their lustful passions are consuming flames. Dante himself receives purification on this terrace again. He passes through a fire of which he says: "I would have flung myself into boiling glass to cool me, so immeasurable was the degree of heat" in the purifying flame. And yet the souls are careful not to step out of the flame, but to keep within its chaste pains and receive its purification. "Blessed are the pure in heart, for they shall see God," is the beatitude directed against lust. To see the eyes of Beatrice, or the Revelation of Divine Theology, Dante must pass through the flame of purification and become pure in heart. So Virgil, in the midst of the flames, discourses of Beatrice to encourage Dante.

§ 23. *The Terrestrial Paradise*

In the Terrestrial Paradise, which is the place of transfigured and perfected human society on earth, Dante finds the Church. It is a complex symbol bodying forth the visible Church [1] and its history (as commentary has sufficiently shown).

---

[1] The seven candlesticks denoting the seven gifts of the Holy Spirit; the seven bands of color streaming out from them, the sacraments, or else the influences of the gifts; the ten paces, the ten commandments; the twenty-four elders, the twenty-four books of the Old Testament crowned with the lilies of faith; the four beasts (*quattro animali*) crowned with green leaves, the four Gospels clad in the color of hope (or salvation); the six wings of protection extending in the six possible directions in space, and full of eyes for providential guardianship (? or perhaps the wings denote inspiration and the eyes the fullness of divine vision); the car of the visible Church in their midst, on two wheels, the

After Dante beholds the history of the Church symbolized and its future prophesied, great empha-
old and the new dispensations, or, rather, as the wheels serve as the means by which the Church moves forward, they signify revelation and tradition (Philalethes), or the priesthood and the monks (Witte); the griffon with his two bodies signifies the divine-human founder of the Church; the lion's body, colored white (faith) and vermilion (charity or grace), symbolizes the human part, and the eagle's head and wings of gold the divine part, the wings rising so high that their ends cannot be seen, extending as they do into the mystic and incomprehensible Godhead; the wings, one of justice and the other of mercy, rise through the bands of influence that stream from the candlesticks, including one sacrament — that of repentance — between the wings as the most essential one of Purgatory, and three sacraments on each side of both wings; the griffon draws the car by its shaft, the cross, and attaches it to a tree, — a tree that suggests the tree of knowledge of good and evil in Paradise, and yet it would seem that Dante refers to the fixing of the papal seat at Rome. Three dames — white, green, and red, to signify the three celestial virtues, faith, hope, and charity — dance by the side of the right wheel; while four dames, clad in purple, to signify the four cardinal or secular virtues, one of whom (Prudence) has three eyes (counsel, agreement, and habit), dance by the left wheel. Then follow the symbols of the remaining books of the New Testament, — St. Luke (of Acts), Saints Paul, Peter, John, James, and Jude for their epistles; a solitary old man sleeping, but with subtle countenance, for Revelation. Beatrice now descends crowned with olive (peace) over a white veil (faith), in a green mantle (hope), and clad in the color of a living flame (love). She signifies divine theology or

sis being placed on its relations to the Empire, he passes through the waters of Lethe, and becomes oblivious of his mortal defects.

§ 24. *The Spiritual Sense of Lethe*

That Lethe is an essential product of the process of purification must be obvious to every one who reflects upon the nature of it. The river of for-

revelation (Scartazzini), or grace that perseveres (Philalethes), and much else, no doubt, — infinite aspiration of the soul. Dante is upbraided for unfaithfulness to this highest aspiration: he has pursued other aims, sought to capture the leopard ; sought also to explain the world by an inferior philosophy (the *quella scuola ch' hai seguitata e sua dottrina* spoken of in xxxiii. 89, 90, and contrasted with the divine way). The reference to unfaithfulness in Canto xxx. is perhaps the symbolic statement of what is literally named in Canto xxxiii. as a philosophic doctrine, and this seems to be acknowledged by Dante (xxxiii. 92). It was perhaps some doctrine derived from the Arabian commentators like Averrhoës, who inclined toward Pantheism and denied individual immortality to men. In his commentary on Aristotle's psychology, Averrhoës understands " the Philosopher " to prove that man has only a "passive" intellect which perishes at death, while the "active intellect," which is the soul of the world, alone possesses persistent being. This was also the interpretation of Alexander of Aphrodisias. St. Thomas Aquinas's greatest service to Christian Theology is his refutation of this error, which places the principle of individuality in the passive rather than in the active part of the human soul.

getfulness does not destroy or impair in any way the recollection of deeds done in the body, but it changes essentially the quality of that memory. In the Inferno state of the soul, sins had been committed as though they were the special private or personal interest of the individual doer, and their punishment was looked upon as though coming from an alien interest outside of the doer. The memory of the Inferno state of the soul, therefore, would preserve the dualism of the selfish me *versus* the avenging social whole. But Purgatory so eradicates this sense of dualism that it leads the individual to feel that his real essential self — his divine self in fact — is the self embodied in the institutions of civilization. With this insight he comes to see all human history as his own history, and to sympathize with the action of the social whole in relation to the individual. Hence he adopts the action of the social whole as his own essential act, and ignores his own particular rights and wrongs as opposed to the universal right of society. He therefore loses the interest of personal memory in himself, and looks upon his old self as an alien personality quite outside of his new self that has grown as a second nature, a regenerated self, through the struggle of Purgatory. He loves his new life, which is in conformity with the life of civilization and the Divine world-order, and he loves whatever deeds of his old life contributed to forming this new life. This is the bath in the stream Eunoe, which brings to memory the good deeds of the past life. The bath in Lethe is the death of the old life of mere individualism.

Moreover, there is a certain progress in the theoretical mind itself which Dante and his like well know that has an effect in raising the soul above sense and memory into the realm of the intuition of ideas. After any one has thoroughly mastered the scientific knowledge of a given province, he abides by the general symbols that sum up his knowledge in the form of abstract ideas. These indicate to him, not mere dead classifications and mere summaries of observation in the form of statistics, but concrete principles involving both energies and laws, so that they explain not only all the facts and phenomena that are collected in the science, but also furnish a permanent image of the eternal process manifested in the facts and phenomena treated of in the science of which he has become the master.

At this point of insight into principles and their energies and laws which produce the processes of nature and life, the mind contemplates what is essential and therefore necessary, and is thereupon released from the obligation to retain all the data of observation which had to be used at first in order to discover the principle. The facts and data are only a scaffolding useful while the temple was building. The principles, for example, of botany do not depend on the facts and phenomena which have furnished the botanists the data on which they have climbed up to laws and principles. Those data were only illustrations flowing from those principles, and not the causes of the principles themselves. The principles once established and in the mind, those data may drop away as so much scaffolding, for the temple is not built on the scaffolding, but on its own foundation; and, although the scaffold is useful in the process of building, it is now no longer needed. So the facts and the phenomena are the accidental illustrations of the principles which pointed the way to their discovery, and now may be forgotten. The scientific mind bathes in the waters of Lethe, and washes away the memory of facts that once imprisoned it in mechanical theories, or systems of classification, or statistical results.

III. THE PARADISO

§ 25. *The Ascent to Paradise*

DANTE gazes into the eyes of Beatrice [1] (symbolizing Divine Knowledge, Christian Theology,

---

[1] Beatrice may signify *perfecting grace*, as Philalethes thinks, or *Revelation*, as Scartazzini prefers. But Dante himself (in the *Convito*, ii. 13) tells us that he imaged Philosophy under the form of a gentle lady and compassionate, and, after thirty months of study of Boethius, he began to feel the sweetness of this lady so much that his love for her chased away all other thoughts. In chapter ii. of the second Treatise he alludes to Beatrice as the gentle lady of the *Vita Nuova*, and in chapter xvi. he discourses at length on the fair lady Philosophy : "The spirit made me look on a fair lady, in which passage it should be understood that this lady is Philosophy ; a lady full of sweetness, indeed, adorned with modesty, wonderful in her wisdom, the glory of freedom. . . . Whoever desires to see his salvation must look steadfastly into this Lady's eyes : —

" 'Chi veder vuol la salute,
   Faccia che gli occhi d' esta donna miri.'

The eyes of the Lady are her demonstrations which look straight into the eyes of the intellect, enamour the soul, and emancipate it from all fettering conditions."

If one understands by Philosophy what Dante expounds

THE ASCENT TO PARADISE

or Revelation), and now ascends to the celestial spheres. There are ten heavens in all, of which the lowest and nearest to the earth is the heaven of the moon, while the highest heaven is the Empyrean.

The doctrine already alluded to as the fundamental principle of Christianity — to wit, that God is pure form, pure self-distinction, pure consciousness, pure personality — is stated in the following discourse of Beatrice, placed in the first canto of the " Paradiso : " —

in his *Convito*, it signifies the insight into a Divine Reason as First Cause without envy and full of goodness or grace. This doctrine is therefore the same as perfecting grace, and the same as the substance of Revelation. For Reason is divine-human. In the *Paradiso*, Canto xxxi., Beatrice leaves Dante, and St. Bernard takes her place. This, perhaps, means that Philosophy, daughter of God though she be (*Convito*, ii. 13), does not suffice to reveal the mystery of the Trinity. St. Bernard as religious mystic expounds the White Rose of Paradise, symbol of the Invisible Church, corresponding to the Visible Church on the summit of the purgatorial mount. He also conducts him to the vision of the Triune God. It makes no difference whether Beatrice is interpreted as Philosophy if understood in the sense that Dante explains in the *Convito*, or as Divine Theology as unfolded by St. Thomas Aquinas, or as perfecting grace if understood as the illuminating effects of this insight, which is the vision of God, or as Revelation if understood as producing this same vision of God.

"All things, what'er they be,
Have order [1] among themselves, and this is form,
That makes the universe resemble God.
Here do the higher creatures see the footprints
Of the Eternal Power, which is the end
Whereto is made the law already mentioned.
In the order that I speak of are inclined
All natures, by their destinies diverse,
More or less near unto their origin;
Hence they move onward unto ports diverse
O'er the great Sea of being; and each one
With instinct given it which bears it on.
This bears away the fire toward the moon.
This is in mortal hearts the motive power;
This binds together and unites the earth.
Nor only the created things that are
Without intelligence this bow shoots forth,
But those that have both intellect and love.
The Providence that regulates all this
Makes with its light the heaven forever quiet,
Wherein that turns which has the greatest haste." [2]

[1] Order is the technical expression for dependence of the lower beings on the Highest, and for the revelation of the Power of the Highest in the lower. In the *Convito* (iii. 7) Dante quotes from the " Book of Causes:" " The First Goodness sends His good gifts forth upon things in one stream." Each thing, adds he, receives from this stream according to the mode of its powers (*virtu*) and its nature. And, again (iv. 8), he quotes St. Thomas as saying, " To know the order of one thing to another is the proper act of Reason." To perceive dependencies in nature is to perceive unity, and therefore to perceive the " Form that makes the universe resemble God."

[2] Longfellow, i. 103–123.

The lowest rests on the highest, and not the highest on the lowest. Things are substantial just in proportion to their degree of participation in the divine self-activity. The lack of self-activity appears as external impulsion and fate to finite things.

The doctrine of ten heavens draws its artificial form from the doctrine of the pseudo-Dionysius concerning the Celestial Hierarchy, and will be considered under the subject of Dante's Mythology. For the present we will limit our attention to the ethical contents of the several heavens in their order.

§ 26. *The Heaven of the Moon, or the Ritualists*

Beatrice fixes her eyes on the Sun — *i. e.* draws light from Theology ("luce virtuosissima Filosofia"),[1] and by this means elevates herself to the heaven of the moon, Dante following by the light reflected from her eyes: —

> "It seemed to me a cloud encompassed us,
> Luminous, dense, consolidate, and bright
> As adamant on which the sun is striking.
> Into itself did the eternal pearl
> Receive us, as water doth receive
> A ray of light, remaining still unbroken.
> If I was body (and we here conceive not
> How one dimension tolerates another,

[1] *Convito,* iv. 1.

> Which needs must be if body enter body),
> More the desire should be enkindled in us
> That essence to behold, wherein is seen
> How God and our own nature were united."[1]

They enter the substance of the moon realizing the fact that one dimension tolerates another. For in spiritual things all may participate without diminution of shares, while in material things there is exclusion and division. Dante beholds the outlines of faces prompt to speak, but they seem so much like reflections that he supposes them to be "mirrored semblances," and looks around to see the persons that are thus reflected. Beatrice corrects his error, and assures him that these are real souls assigned to the sphere of the moon for the breaking of some vow.

They were forced by external influences to break their vows, but had their wills been firm unto death they would not have been compelled. This heaven of the moon, therefore, holds souls who have attained heaven, but with some defect of will. In a discourse on the nature of heaven, it is explained to Dante that everywhere in heaven is Paradise, and that each soul belongs to all the heavens, although he will behold the special heavens filled each with souls of a certain rank or degree, in order to teach him that there are different

[1] Longfellow, ii. 31–42.

degrees of celestial growth, notwithstanding each one has access to all the heavens.

The moon was known to Dante to shine with reflected light, and to be nearest to the earth. The moon also presents phases, waxing and waning because of relation to another light. Moreover, it has dark and light spots on its surface. It, therefore, is a proper symbol for the heaven that contains those souls who have willed in conformity to the divine will, but intermittently and in a formal manner, or who have not willed supremely the divine. Hence they are fittingly placed here in the moon, and appear as though reflections and not substances. Inasmuch as their obedience to prescribed forms and ceremonies of the Church is very nearly mechanical, and not from genuine insight, you can scarcely distinguish their actuality from the reflection of somebody else's will in which they appear. He who made the forms and ceremonies, and who taught them how to perform them, lives in them still as their reality, — they manifest his will rather than their own freedom. If they happen to be derelict from lack of firmness of will, yielding to others who assume authority over them, their course resembles still more the inconstancy of the moon, as appears in its changes. The spirits of the formal order show inconstancy and instability, therefore, because they appear and disappear in the will of another, according as it interrupts or changes its relation to them by some external circumstance. And we must supply this natural inference to Dante's picture, and see in these lunar souls not only the interposition of violent family authority, as in the case of Piccarda, dragged away from monastic vows by her brother, Corso Donati, but also the lunar variations of temperament, moods, and external conditions.

§ 27. *The Heavens of Imperfect Wills*

The heavens of imperfect wills include also those of Mercury and Venus. We must keep in mind this distinction between true and spurious individuality. The true individuality energizes to produce for itself and within itself, and also on the world, the divine form of God's will. The more completely it does this, the more completely it fills itself with divine freedom, and thus becomes independent, or symbolically able to shine by its own light, for its own light arises from energizing according to the divine form. The spurious individuality arises from intermingling any kind or variety of selfishness between itself and the divine, — or, in other words, from acting with partial or entire reference to itself instead of the divine.

In the moon the will does not cast life into the scale, but lets love of life determine its actions in a last resort. Besides, it acts wholly from another's insight even when it obeys the divine commands.

§ 28. *The Pusillanimous, the Procrastinators, and the Formalists*

The correspondence between these spirits of the moon and the pusillanimous ones on the shore of Acheron will not fail to strike us. They had no choice of their own, but went where the wasps and hornets of chance and circumstance impelled them. The souls who have procrastinated repentance until the last moment likewise are placed on the outer terrace of Purgatory, and not allowed to enter St. Peter's gate. The pusillanimous, the procrastinators, and the mechanical formalists are found on the outer verges of the three worlds. But, although formalists, these souls sacrifice their inclinations for the service of the Church, and are in Paradise, though immature in spiritual insight.

§ 29. *The Heaven of Mercury. The Love of Fame*

In the Heaven of Mercury, the love of fame prevents the perfect devotion of the hero to a divine cause. Perfect devotion would elevate him to Mars or Jupiter. The Mercurial saint does not abandon himself to the cause for itself alone, but only as moved by a love of fame.

Fame is the reflection, not of the deed itself, shining in us as inspired by the deepest conviction, but the reflection of the deed shining in the recognition of our fellow-men. This destroys or affects our freedom. We have not the true celestial revolution derived from the *Primum Mobile*, but a defective sort of orbit, — an epicycle in fact.

The planets Mercury and Venus move in epicycles. They drive out of their course in order to move round the sun as they pass through the zodiac. They never get far away from the sun, but pass through the zodiac only because the sun in his course carries them around it. They act, not from an independent purpose of their own, to complete the course of the celestial revolution of themselves. The sun is the great luminary of day, symbolizing the spiritual light as well. Hence it not improperly means fame for Mercury.

Mercury is usually eclipsed by the sun's rays, and is rarely ever seen because of its closeness to the sun. So, too, in case of the Mercurial saint, we cannot tell how much he is moved by his own insight into what is holy, and how much he is impelled by the fame attached to the cause that he engages in. It is his cause that ennobles him, and we do not know how much to subtract from him on account of his selfish ambition. The sun of his cause is to be accredited with much of his action.

The true hero, who devotes himself with utter self-abnegation to his cause, shines independently. We shall see this species of hero in the heaven of Mars. The cause shines in him, and not he in the cause. He does not use it as a semi-external means of fame, but he becomes the cause itself, and his individuality widens to the greatness of independent subsistence. Ambition conflicts with Divine Charity in the heaven of Mercury.[1]

[1] Dante introduces Justinian in Mercury (Canto vi.), in order to give the history of Rome and show its providential place in the world. It is full of conflicts between ambition and pure patriotism, and suits well to this heaven of Mercury. Under the Empire, vengeance was done on Calvary for the ancient sin in the Garden of Eden, and later, under Titus, another vengeance was done upon that vengeance by the destruction of Jerusalem. Providence, having selected Rome as the residence of the head of the Church, "will not change his scutcheon for the lilies." France must bethink herself of this. The allusion of Justinian to a just vengeance that could be justly avenged gives occasion (Canto vii.) for a discourse from Beatrice on Incarnation and Immortality, in which Aristotle's doctrine of the goodness of God ("without envy") is used after the manner of the Schoolmen St. Thomas and Hugo of St. Victor. Divine condescension and human freedom are dwelt upon. Supreme beneficence lifts man into the rank of immortals. Here is the ground of the human desire for fame, infinite aspiration founded on the divine gift of immortality, and the divine election of man to a union with God.

§ 30. *The Heaven of Venus. Love as Limited to Special Spheres*

The Heaven of Venus is also a heaven of imperfect will. It is that of lovers, and includes the conjugal, the parental, the filial, and the fraternal, as well as the love of friends. Terrestrial love is connected with a limitation, — devoted to a special object, parent, child, husband, wife, brother, sister, or friend. Such love is of the same nature fundamentally as celestial love or Divine Charity. But there is a particular limitation in the former which prevents its complete identity.

The planet Venus is not obscured by the sun's rays to the same extent as Mercury. It gives notice of the rising sun as Lucifer, and it follows the setting sun as Hesperus. It is "brightest of all the starry host," but is not independent of the sun. It reveals and celebrates the sun rising or setting, — the friendly herald and disciple. It is dependent on the sun, moving in an epicycle round it. As represented in the charming Auroras of Guido and Guercino, it looks back lovingly to the King of Day.

But it is not the love of St. Francis of Assisi, not the divine charity displayed by the Poor in Spirit, devoted to the resurrection of the divine spirit in those who most need it, — the dregs and scum of humanity. It is not willing to be crucified in order that it may save them.

The theory of Copernicus, to which we are accustomed, is, of course, very different from the astronomy of Dante, and, we may add, not so well adapted for the poetic use he makes of the solar and stellar systems. Dante deals with the starry heavens as they appear to actual observation. The theory of Copernicus exists only for our reason, and is not a poetic matter. According to Ptolemy, the moon shines by reflected light, but not so the planets. Their phases could not be perceived without the aid of a telescope. The inferior planets seemed to Dante to revolve primarily around the sun, and to accompany him around the zodiac; while the superior planets — Mars, Jupiter, and Saturn — seemed to revolve around the zodiac independently, like the sun itself.

Terrestrial love moves in the direction of the divine love, but in channels with high banks, so that it acts with regard to a few, and intermits in regard to many. It is allied to selfishness in the fact that it is thus limited to those near it, or connected by natural ties. It is therefore imperfect in the manner symbolized by Dante. It possesses, like the planet Venus, an individuality, but an individuality that is ancillary, — subordinated to another. Terrestrial love has so much of the true celestial individuality that it can appear independently (*i. e.* shine by its own light), but its course is back and forth along the heavenly pathway, and not always progressive.

§ 31. *The Heaven of the Sun. Theologians*

The fourth heaven, or that of the sun, forms the transition from the lower to the higher order of heavens.

It is the heaven of theologians. The doctrine of the Trinity, as taught by the Church, is the dogmatic version of the doctrine of divine form laid down by Beatrice in the first canto. It is the doctrine that explains how an infinitely perfect being creates a finite, imperfect being.

The tenth canto begins with the doctrine of the Holy Spirit: —

> "Looking into his Son with all the Love
> Which each of them eternally breathes forth,
> The primal and unutterable Power
> Whate'er before the mind or eye revolves
> With so much order made, there can be none
> Who this beholds without enjoying it." [1]

Dante's love of theology has led him to this heaven, and he is filled with gratitude to God for his goodness in raising him to this place.

In this great family of theologians he finds not

[1] Longfellow, x. 1–6.

only Thomas Aquinas and Albertus Magnus, but also Dionysius the Areopagite and the mystics, Richard of St. Victor, and St. Bonaventura. In this heaven St. Thomas narrates the life of St. Francis, who wedded poverty or humility — Poverty in Spirit had been a widow since the crucifixion. Afterward, St. Bonaventura recounts the deeds of St. Dominic. St. Francis and St. Dominic are the two great reformers of Monasticism in the thirteenth century. They moved out to conquer the world, the Franciscans preaching to the poor and lowly; the Dominicans teaching the governing classes of society, and cultivating literature and theology. Each is celebrated here by the mouth of the other's most eminent disciple.

In the heaven of the sun we hear from St. Thomas the wisdom of Solomon, — the doctrine of the Word and the Spirit and the nine subsistences. All things are but the thought of God and created by him in love.

> "That which can die, and that which dieth not,
> Are nothing but the splendor of the idea
> Which by his love our Lord brings into being;
> Because that living Light which from its fount
> Effulgent flows, so that it disunites not
> From Him nor from the Love in them intrined,
> Through its own goodness reunites its rays
> In nine subsistences, as in a mirror,
> Itself eternally remaining One.

> Thence it descends to the last potencies,
> Downward from act to act becoming such
> That only brief contingencies it makes;
> And these contingencies I hold to be
> Things generated, which the heaven produces
> By its own motion, with seed and without.
> Neither their wax, nor that which tempers it,
> Remains immutable, and hence beneath
> The ideal signet more and less shines through;
> Therefore it happens that the self-same tree
> After its kind bears worse and better fruit,
> And ye are born with characters diverse.
> If in perfection tempered were the wax,
> And were the heaven in its supremest virtue,
> The brilliance of the seal would all appear;
> But nature gives it evermore deficient,
> In the like manner working as the artist,
> Who has the skill of art and hand that trembles.
> If then the fervent Love, the Vision clear,
> Of primal Virtue do dispose and seal,
> Perfection absolute is there acquired."[1]

Herein we have a new statement of the Form which makes the universe resemble God. It is an account of the rise of finite, imperfect beings. In God, says St. Thomas, knowing and willing are one, so that his consciousness of himself — his knowing of himself on the part of "Primal Virtue" — creates another, the "Vision Clear." From these two proceed the Third Person, the "Fervent Love." The Trinity was denied by Sabellius, and on leaving this heaven of divine theology it is fit-

[1] Longfellow, xiii. 52–81.

ting that we have the great heresiarchs condemned by the mouth of St. Thomas. But a caution is added:—

> "Nor yet shall people be too confident
> In judging, even as he is who doth count
> The corn in field or ever it be ripe.
> For I have seen all winter long the thorn
> First show itself intractable and fierce,
> And after bear the rose upon its top;
> And I have seen a ship direct and swift
> Run o'er the sea throughout its course entire
> To perish at the harbor's mouth at last.
> . . . .
> Let not Dame Bertha nor Ser Martin think,
> Seeing one steal, another offering make,
> To see in them the arbitrament divine;
> For one may rise, and fall the other may."

§ 32. *The Heaven of Mars. True Heroes*

In the fifth heaven are found the great Christian heroes and martyrs who have risked their lives from zeal for the true faith. These are arranged in the form of a cross stretched athwart the sky, on which Christ is flashing, symbolic of the spirit of self-sacrifice which is dominant in the character of these Martial saints. These are not those heroes who were obscured by love of fame like the Mercurial saints, but the firm in will and deep in faith. Here Dante listens to the long discourse from Cacciaguida concerning the good old times in Florence.[1] In this heaven of the true spirit of patriotism and heroic self-sacrifice for principle, the poet naturally recurs to the subject nearest his heart, and through the mouth of his ancestor he describes the old order and the genesis of the new. The remedy for the evils in Italy in a firmly seated imperial power is prophetically indicated. Thus Dante comes again to the burning question ("Convito," fourth Treatise) at every possible opportunity. The subject is continued in the next heaven, to which we now arrive.

§ 33. *The Heaven of Jupiter. Righteous Kings*

In the sixth heaven, that of Jupiter, we find the righteous kings arranged in the form of an enormous Eagle, — symbol of the Holy Roman Empire.

As we rise from heaven to heaven in the Paradise, we reach a more adequate state of devotion of the individual to the welfare of the social whole. Each one unites with his fellows to produce an aggregate social result. This is symbolized by the formation of great figures out of saints arranged, as in Mars, so as to present a colossal cross; or, in Jupiter, so as to spell out the words that express ethical principles, or to present a great Eagle, or, in the tenth heaven, the Rose of Paradise. This paradise is the state of those whose deeds reinforce society.

[1] Cantos xv.–xviii.

§ 34. *The Doctrine of Salvation*

The Eagle discourses of salvation by faith, and touches on the important question of the salvation of the heathen: —

> "For saidst thou: 'Born a man is on the shore
> Of Indus, and is none who there can speak
> Of Christ, nor who can read, nor who can write;
> And all his inclinations and his actions
> Are good, so far as human reason sees,
> Without a sin in life or in discourse:
> He dieth unbaptized and without faith?
> Where is this justice that condemneth him?
> Where is his fault, if he do not believe?'
> Now who art thou, that on the bench wouldst sit
> In judgment at a thousand miles away,
> With the short vision of a single span?"[1]

This, of course, shuts out the exercise of human reason. While it is true that our failure to comprehend the total system renders it impossible for us to condemn divine justice in a single instance, yet, on the other hand, we are called upon to understand as far as possible the purposes of Providence, and to see their supreme reasonableness. This we may do in given instances, and probably in all, if we ponder the subject sufficiently. Only our negative judgments are insufficient; where the divine decree seems irrational, there we may be sure that we do not comprehend the case. If we

---

[1] Longfellow, xix. 70–81.

are sure of the existence of the decree as a fact, we are sure of its rationality, on the same ground that Dante's philosophy assures him of the existence of God. Form and order — the dependence of all things in space and time — unite everything to every other; it is the universal relativity of which we hear so much in natural philosophy. This interdependence proves the unity of the whole; and accordingly the whole in all its changes, in all its beginnings and its ceasings, manifests one sole energy, — an energy of self-determination whose form is Reason, — Νόησις νοήσεως, as Aristotle calls it. Since the Absolute is self-related, and can only be self-related, from its very nature its self-knowing will result in other creatures. Because that divine knowing, in making itself an object, generates another like itself, — the eternal Word as the eternal thought of the eternal Reason. This is the doctrine of the Logos, and was understood by Plato and Aristotle, though not stated by the latter in the same terms as by Plato. It was seen clearly by these two philosophers that the necessary dependence (*ordo*) of things in space implies or presupposes an Absolute; that the relative presupposes an independent, self-related Absolute. It was seen, in the second place, that the Absolute has necessarily the form of self-activity or self-determination, and that self-activity in its perfect

THE DOCTRINE OF SALVATION 97

form is Reason, subject and object in one. Following this a third step, they saw that such an absolute Reason is perfect goodness, or without envy (see Canto vii., "La divina bontà, che da sè sperne ogni livore "),[1] and this is explicitly stated by both

[1] *Livore*, used in this passage (vii. 65), also used in *Purgatorio*, xiv. 84, names envy by its livid hue. Without doubt this word is suggested to Dante by Boethius, who indeed suggests also this whole passage in regard to the divine goodness. In *The Consolation of Philosophy*, Metrum ix. of the third book, he speaks of "the form of the supreme goodness, devoid of envy, not impelled to create by external causes" (*verum insita summi forma boni livore carens*). To Boethius is due also the form of the *Vita Nuova*, and especially that of the *Convito*. For Boethius puts in verse the substance of a prose discourse in each chapter. Dante makes his prose discourse a commentary on the verse, while Boethius makes the latter a summary. In the old translation of Boethius "by the Right Honorable Richard Lord Viscount Preston" (London, 1695) is the following rendering of the first portion of Metrum ix.: —

> "O thou who with perpetual Reason rul'st
> The World, great Maker of the Heaven and Earth!
> Who dost from ages make swift Time proceed,
> And fix'd thyself, mak'st all things else to move!
> Whom exterior Causes did not force to frame
> This Work of floating Matter, but the Form
> Of Sovereign Good, above black Envy plac'd,
> Within thy Breast; thou everything dost draw
> From the supreme Example; fairest thyself,
> Bearing the World's Figure in thy Mind,
> Thou formedst this after that Prototype," etc.

When we go back to Dante and to the Christian writers

philosophers.[1] In other words, this is the doctrine that Creation proceeds from God's grace. He desires to share his life with other beings without number ("Convito," Second Treatise, ch. v., "He has made spiritual creatures innumerable").

The doctrine of the Logos includes a further thought, and from this is derived the idea of creation and the procession of the Holy Spirit. If Divine Reason, in thinking itself as object, causes that object to exist as its perfect other, — an eternally and only begotten, — it follows that the only begotten Logos is a perfect reason ($\nu\acute{o}\eta\sigma\iota\varsigma\ \nu o\acute{\eta}\sigma\epsilon\omega\varsigma$) who also causes his own object to exist independently. The Logos in knowing himself has to know himself as independent and perfect, and also to know himself as begotten, as derived from the First Reason (not as *being* derived, but as one who has completed his derivation and become perfect). His knowledge of his perfection makes for its

of earlier ages, we find their statements taking on the technical terms in which this great doctrine of divine Goodness was stated by the philosophy of Plato and Aristotle. The creed had not at that time become a mere formula of words confessed to have no meaning that can be comprehended, but it was a "symbolum" or statement of the highest insight attained by the contemplative souls within the Church ("Symbolum est professio fidei," Thomas Aquinas, *Summa Theologica*, ii. 2, article ix.).

[1] *Timæus*, 29, and *Metaphors*, Book I. ch. ii.

object the Holy Spirit; and his knowledge of his derivation creates a world of derivation or evolution containing all stages in it of growth and development, from chaos or unformed matter below up to the highest saint or angel above. Space and time are the forms of all finite existence; they condition matter. The universe in time and space is the *Processio* of the Holy Ghost. Nature is the process of creating conscious, rational souls who — being arrived at the doctrine of Christianity, " the good of the Intellect,"[1] the doctrine of God as pure grace — set up charity as the highest principle, and form an Invisible Church which is the " Rose of Paradise," — innumerable souls united through brotherly helpfulness, so that each prefers the welfare of all others to his own, and by such altruism becomes the recipient of the providential care of all. Such an Invisible Church, including all rational beings in all the worlds in space, and especially the infinitely numerous spirits that have passed through death to immortality, is celebrated in the Apocalypse as the " Bride." This Invisible Church has one spirit, because mutual interdependence makes unity, — it is an institutional Spirit, — The Holy Spirit.

The form of this statement is different from that of Dante and St. Thomas, and from that of

[1] Aristotle.

the mystics, but is substantially their view. If one will take this view in its history, beginning with Plato and Aristotle and following it down to Philo and Alexandrian mysticism, — beginning again with the New Testament statements of it by St. John in his Gospel and by St. Paul in Colossians,[1] trace its growth in the creeds through the conflict with Arianism, and finally through the conflict of the Greek and Roman churches, — he will find this statement a clue to the entire movement and the mysterious principle that guided the church fathers in defining their *symbola* as well as in building up their systems of theology. Interpreted by this, one may see the general ethical significance of the expression "faith in Christ," as a faith in the doctrine of grace and the recognition of divine charity as the highest principle.

> "It recommenced : ' Unto this kingdom never
> Ascended one who had not faith in Christ,
> Before or since he to the tree was nailed.
> But look thou, many crying are, "Christ, Christ!"
> Who at the judgment shall be far less near
> To him than some shall be who knew not Christ.' "[2]

Interpreting this by the doctrine of the Logos as above stated, all beings in the world, conscious and unconscious, are created by the act of the

[1] i. 13–20.   [2] Longfellow, xix. 103–108.

Logos. He recognizes his derivation; whatever he knows as object he causes to exist as object. Man may think a thought without causing it to exist; his will is different from his knowing; this constitutes man's finitude; but in God will and intellect are one.[1] Hence, whatever God knows he gives existence, and whatever finitude exists, exists in the knowledge of the Logos. Individual existence is, therefore, derived from grace which gives separate subsistence to that which is finite and imperfect. But such imperfect or finite exists only in a state of change and genesis, for it is the thought of his own genesis that causes the finite to exist — it exists only in a state of becoming or evolution. Hence it is said in theology that all improvement and growth in intellect and morality is a work of grace. Hence, too, it is said that Christ bears the sins of men; he thinks all their imperfections, and does not annihilate them because of imperfection. He is the Mediator with the First Person because the First thinks perfection and generates a Perfect Logos. To think imperfection, God must find it in some way involved with his being. The Logos, inasmuch as there is derivation or generation logically im-

---

[1] "In Deo sit idem voluntas et intellectus." St. Thomas Aquinas, *Summa Theologica*, I. q. xxvii. art. 3. See, also, *Contra Gentiles*, lib. iv. cap. 19.

plied in his being, necessarily thinks imperfection, but only as a preface and procession toward perfection. He is perfection, and no imperfection remains in the Logos; but there is a logical implication that there was such imperfection in the fact that he was begotten or derived from the First. This logical derivation necessary to the thought of his relation to the First becomes a real derivation in time and space. But the thought of finitude and imperfection must be looked upon as repugnant to the mind of the Logos, and to be endured only in view of what proceeds from it. In religious symbolism he is spoken of as redeeming finite beings through his incarnation and death on the Cross. This expresses symbolically the act of the Logos in Creation. For the sake of reconciliation or atonement, and the existence of the invisible Church of believers in divine charity, God creates matter and lower forms of being, and educes, from these, higher and higher forms of self-activity and freedom, culminating in immortal souls who may freely unite in institutions. Institutions enable each member to reap the united result of the whole. Philosophy must certainly agree with religion in this: that the existence of matter and lower forms of life — not only these, but the higher and highest forms of life and finite spirit — are evidences of benevolent goodness (grace) in

THE DOCTRINE OF SALVATION

the First Principle. Nature seems even to the scientist (illuminated by the thought of Darwin) to be a vast process of developing individuality. For the fittest survives, and the fittest is the most able to conquer by ideas. All matter struggles to assume the form of man, or, —

> "Striving to be man, the worm
> Mounts through all the spires of form."

Souls may exist without this doctrine, but they are not in the Paradise and the Holy Spirit does not dwell in them. They are, however, subject to conversion by the spirits who have found the truth.

The voice of the spirit choir, seeming to proceed from the beak of the Eagle, continues its discourse, and Dante is informed that the supreme saints forming the eye are the supreme saints of this heaven, David the psalmist being its very pupil.

"Of the five who make me a circle for eyelid, he who is closest beside my beak consoled the poor widow for her son. Now knows he how dear it costs not to follow Christ by the experience of this sweet life and of the opposite." [1]

This was the Emperor Trajan, the story of whose justice so interested St. Gregory that he interceded with prayers for his soul, and, having his bones disinterred, baptized him and thus

[1] Butler, xx. 43–48.

brought him into Paradise. This shows the power of the Church over the souls in the Limbo. But Dante carries it a step further by saving on his own authority the soul of Rhipeus, whom Virgil has called the justest of all that were in Troy.[1] Dante makes him one of the five supreme spirits in the eye of the Eagle.

"Who would believe down in the erring world that Rhipeus of Troy should be in this round the fifth of the holy lights? Now knows he enough of that which the world cannot see of the divine grace, albeit his view discerns not the depth. Like a lark which goes abroad in air, singing first, and then holds her peace, content with the last sweetness which sates her, such seemed to me the image of the imprint of the eternal pleasure, according to its desire for which each thing becomes of what sort it is. And albeit in that place I was in regard to my doubting as glass to the color which covers it, it did not suffer me to wait awhile in silence, but with the force of its weight it urged from my mouth, 'What things are these?' Wherefore of sparkling I beheld a great festival. Thereafter, with its eye more kindled, the blessed ensign responded to me, not to keep me in suspense wondering : 'I see that thou believest these things because I say them, but seest not how; so that if they are

[1] *Æneid*, ii. 426.

believed, they are concealed. Thou dost as he who well apprehends the thing by name, but its quiddity he cannot see, if another sets it not forth. *Regnum cœlorum* suffereth violence of warm love and of lively hope, which overcomes the divine will, not in such wise as man has the mastery over man, but overcomes it, because it wills to be overcome, and, being overcome, overcomes with its own goodness. The first life in the eyelid and the fifth make thee marvel because with them thou seest the angels' domain adorned.'" [1]

The principle of grace in the Christian religion contains infinite depths yet to be revealed in creeds and practice. The adjustment of the principle of grace to the principle of justice has furnished the most difficult of theological problems. It is the old question of Orientalism as against Occidentalism, — Asia *versus* Europe. The Eagle says that " Rhipeus placed all his love below upon righteousness, being led by grace that distills from a Fountain so deep that never creature has been able to see its first wave; from grace to grace God opened his eye to our future redemption." Then, with this example of salvation, he concludes with a warning against the sin of limiting in thought God's grace: —

[1] Butler, xx. 67–102.

> "O thou predestination, how remote
> Thy root is from the aspect of all those
> Who the First Cause do not behold entire!
> And you, O mortals! hold yourselves restrained
> In judging; for ourselves, who look on God,
> We do not know as yet all the elect." [1]

§ 35. *The Heaven of Saturn*

The seventh heaven, that of Saturn, is said to be the special place for the contemplative spirits, — the highest mystics. But while we find St. Bonaventura and Dionysius in the heaven of the sun with Albert and St. Thomas, here are found only St. Peter Damiano and St. Benedict; and the former does not speak of highest and subtlest doctrines, but only inveighs against the luxury of modern prelates, while the latter complains of the corruption of the monks.

The eighth heaven is that of the fixed stars to which Dante follows Beatrice, beholding the solar system at such a distance that the planets seemed to form a small cluster of stars. Here he beholds the Triumph of Christ.

Dante is now examined by St. Peter on the subject of Faith (xxiv.), by St. James on that of Hope (xxv.), and by St. John on that of Charity (xxvi.).

One looks for a mystical interpretation for these three celestial virtues from Dante in this place, or

[1] Longfellow, xx. 130-135.

at least for hints of such an interpretation. What he finds at first is the ordinary definitions taken in the ordinary sense. "Faith is the substance of things hoped for and the evidence of things not seen." In what sense can there be a substance (ὑπόστασις) or hypostasis of things hoped for?

Faith is not contrasted with knowledge of the higher order, but only with knowledge attained by experience. Faith is a higher order of knowledge, — a knowledge founded on insight into what is necessarily and eternally true. We know phenomena by sense-perception, but we know noumena through insight into the presuppositions of things that appear to our senses. We perceive things and events by our senses, but we perceive time and space by reflection. Things and events may or may not be, but time and space must be, and cannot be thought away. We may be said to know time and space by faith in this technical sense. Faith is not mere belief founded on probabilities, or on hearsay, though it is often taken in that sense. Probable knowledge does not go for so much as this true faith. Faith in mere hearsay relates to things of sense whose existence is not necessary but contingent. They exist at one time and cease to exist at another, — to-day the lily of the field is, but to-morrow it is withered and gone. But the logical conditions of existence do not pass away, nor are they to be perceived or known by sense-perception.

But Christian faith is something else than mere insight into what is logically permanent. It is insight into the principle of grace as the source of all things, of time and space, as well as things and events. The Trinity is the supreme object of faith, and it is the object of highest knowledge and subtlest insight. Faith is the substance of things hoped for, inasmuch as it explains how human life is a part of an eternal life, a part of the Procession of the Holy Ghost, a career which begins here and ends no more through all the future. All things hoped for or worthy of being hoped for have, therefore, their substance and ground in this doctrine, as the deepest insight attained by the human mind. Faith is "evidence of things not seen" (ἔλεγχος, or "evidence," is proof or conviction) in the general sense of all *a priori* knowledge. All non-sensuous knowledge is of this order. It is not less probable but more probable than sense-knowledge. Sense-knowledge tells us that this or that object undergoes a change; insight tells us that, if it undergoes a change, there is a cause for it: and this is not a probability but a certainty. The observation of the change may have been a mistake, but the insight cannot be. Sense-perception looks for the cause of the change, say of the movement of a piece of matter, and finds it perhaps in an animal, perhaps in another body. But insight knows that a real efficient cause must be found in a self-activity, in a living being, plant, animal, or man, or in God. Sense-perception may be mistaken in identifying any being as cause; but insight, or faith in this high sense of " the evidence of things not seen," cannot be mistaken as to the fact of the existence of a cause of this change or of any change. Moreover, although we may speak truly of plant, animal, or man as a cause, yet the causal energy is invisible and cannot be a matter of sense-perception, which is limited to effects. It sees limbs move, but not the force that moves them. Faith in this sense is, as St. Peter observes, correctly placed among the substances, and also among the proofs (*tra gli argomenti*). " Faith is that capacity of mind " — St. Thomas quotes this definition [1] — " wherein eternal life begins in us, making our intellect assured of invisible beings."

The greatest of all miracles in the world is its adoption of Christianity, says Dante; for that poverty and the doctrine of other-worldliness should turn aside people enjoying this world seems impossible. But Christianity is not so ascetic as Buddhism or Brahminism, which hold more devotees to-day than Christianity. But miracle in religion

[1] ii. 2, qu. 4, art. 1.

has this deep sense as foundation of faith: All manifestation of force is ultimately the manifestation of self-activity. Self-activity is the opposite of mechanism and mechanical links in a chain of causation. The religious mind does not pause for a moment on the mechanical nexus, but flies at once to the efficient cause, — a self-activity.

Dante repeats his "*credo*," but carries it only through the portion that relates to one eternal God in three eternal Persons, distinct as persons but one in essence, so that of them *is* and *are* may both be predicated.

"Hope is a sure expectation of the future glory which is the effect produced by divine grace and preceding merit," is Dante's reply[1] to the holy catechist. It is not hope in the ordinary sense, but hope based on the faith or insight into the constitution of the universe, — a faith based on the knowledge of God and the Final Cause of His Creation. It is thus, as St. Thomas explains it, "a sure expectation of future glory." It is to the will what faith is to the intellect.[2] With the inequalities of insight and the vicissitudes of life, Hope supports the soul during its nights and eclipses, giving steadfastness to the will.

The approach of St. John temporarily eclipses

[1] Quoted from Peter the Lombard, as Philalethes shows.
[2] St. Thomas Aquinas, *Summa Theologica*, ii. 2, qu. 18.

Beatrice by excess of light. To his catechist Dante defines the object of love as God, and affirms that he has learned this through Philosophy (Plato and Aristotle teaching him that the divine is without envy), and also from revelation. Love is the foundation of all Being. One may have faith (insight) or hope, and yet not admit the divine principle into his heart. But with divine charity he becomes filled with it and is it.

Dante now is permitted to see Adam the archetypal man, for he has fulfilled the course of human education, having passed his examination in this heaven of Saturn, highest of the planets or varying stars.

St. Peter, however (as a sort of favor to Dante?), takes occasion to administer a violent rebuke to certain of his successors in the papal chair.

§ 36. *The Heaven of the Fixed Stars*

Dante and Beatrice now leave the solar system and ascend to the heaven of the fixed stars, — the *primum mobile*, or first moved; for motion is communicated to all the lower heavens by this heaven which is the crystalline sphere. The unmoved heaven, the tenth, is the Empyrean. Spiritual perfection ($\dot{\epsilon}\nu\tau\epsilon\lambda\acute{\epsilon}\chi\epsilon\iota\alpha$) is all in all, and everywhere perfect. But that which is in space and time is sundered, so that it is not everywhere self-identical. But the imperfect desires to be perfect. It is part real and part potential; hence it moves in order to realize its potentialities. Hence change in the world is caused by desire on the part of that which is imperfect to realize all its potentialities and become perfect. This is Aristotle's theory of the movements and changes in the world, and especially of the stars. If each point in space could be all points at once, it would reach perfection. This it attempts to do through movement. (This thought of Aristotle and also of Plato — at first seemingly whimsical — will bear the closest examination. It is an interesting fact that Hegel adopts it in his " Naturphilosophie "). The *primum mobile*, or crystalline sphere, " desires " to touch the Empyrean in each and every part at once with all its own parts, and thus have perfect contact. Hence it moves with inconceivable swiftness, so that this contact shall occur with the least possible intervals of delay.

The Empyrean is all-living flame (symbol of pure self-activity). It is everywhere total and complete, just as the soul is everywhere present in the body in the act of feeling. " And this is why," says Dante in the " Convito,"[1] " that first moved — the *Primum Mobile* — has such extremely rapid

[1] Second Treatise, chap. iv. E. P. Sayer's translation.

motion; for, because of the most fervent appetite which each part of it has to be united with each part of that most divine heaven of peace, in which it revolves with so much desire, its velocity is almost incomprehensible."

Dante learns here of the nine hierarchies. Beatrice discourses also of the creation of the angels and of the fall of Lucifer: —

> "Jerome has written unto you of angels
> Created a long lapse of centuries
> Or ever yet the other world was made;
> But written is this truth in many places
> By writers of the Holy Ghost, and thou
> Shalt see it, if thou lookest well thereat,
> And even reason seeth it somewhat,
> For it would not concede that for so long
> Could be the motors without their perfection."[1]

The higher has its perfection in giving help and guidance to the lower, and hence is not without the lower.

> "Nor could one reach, in counting, unto twenty
> So swiftly, as a portion of these angels
> Disturbed the subject of your elements.
> The rest remained, and they began this art
> Which thou discernest, with so great delight
> That never from their circling do they cease.
> The occasion of the fall was the accursed
> Presumption of that One whom thou hast seen
> By all the burden of the world constrained."[2]

[1] Longfellow, xxix. 37-45.
[2] Ibid., xxix. 49-57.

In describing the angels the subject of angelic knowing (treated of elsewhere in this essay) is touched upon.[1] "They behold God's face direct, and therefore naught is hidden from them." For they look into universals and behold in the efficient and final causes the entire compass of effects. "Their vision is not interrupted by new objects, and hence they have no need to remember through partial concepts." They do not know by objects which, though real, yet are defective in that they do not exhibit all the possibilities of their species; for example, by the senses I see this oak, which is only one specimen out of a multitude. Scientific knowing so reinforces my sense-perception by the sense-perception of all men that I may come to see in this oak all oaks, or, rather, I may compare it with the species and note its defects.

Beatrice improves the occasion to reprehend vehemently that sort of theologians and preachers who have, through ignorance or avarice, substituted inventions of their own for the truth.

They now ascend to the highest heaven, — the tenth, — and Dante sees the river of light of the Empyrean and the White Rose of Paradise, in which all the souls of all the heavens find their place, the Paradise being symbolized by this perfect participation of each in the whole.

[1] Longfellow, xxix. 79.

Beatrice futher discusses the ignorance and
avarice of the clergy, and also hints of the sale
of indulgences, supplementing St. Peter's condemnation of higher dignitaries.

§ 37. *The Empyrean. The White Rose of Paradise. The Vision of God*

In the tenth heaven Dante beholds the river of light: —

> "And light I saw in fashion of a river
> Fulvid with its effulgence, 'twixt two banks
> Depicted with an admirable Spring.
> Out of this river issued living sparks,
> And on all sides sank down into the flowers,
> Like unto rubies that are set in gold;
> And then, as if inebriate with the odors,
> They plunged again into the wondrous torrent,
> And as one entered, issued forth another." [1]

This river takes the form of the White Rose of Paradise: —

> "Thus into greater pomp were changed for me
> The flowerets and the sparks, so that I saw
> Both of the Courts of Heaven made manifest. . . .
> There is a light above, which visible
> Makes the Creator unto every creature,
> Who only in beholding Him has peace,
> And it expands itself in circular form
> To such extent that its circumference
> Would be too large a girdle for the sun. . . .

[1] Longfellow, xxx. 61–69.

> And as a hill in water at its base
> Mirrors itself, as if to see its beauty
> When affluent most in verdure and in flowers,
> So, ranged aloft all around about the light,
> Mirrored I saw in more ranks than a thousand
> All who above there have from us returned." [1]

> "Into the Yellow of the Rose Eternal
> That spreads, and multiplies, and breathes an odor
> Of praise unto the ever-vernal Sun."

Beatrice drew him as if she fain would speak, and said: —

> "Behold how vast the circuit of our city!
> Behold our seats so filled to overflowing,
> That here henceforward are few people wanting!" [2]

Dante compares his vision of the rose to the vision of a barbarian who has come from some remote region, and now "beholds Rome and all her noble works:" —

> "I, who to the divine had from the human,
> From time unto eternity, had come
> From Florence to a people just and sane,
> With what amazement must I have been filled!"

He turns round to question Beatrice concerning this wonderful sight, but she has vanished and taken her place as a petal in the great white rose, and Dante finds an old man robed in glory by his side, who has been summoned by Beatrice to aid him. It is St. Bernard. After explaining the

---

[1] Longfellow, xxx. 94–114.
[2] Ibid., xxx. 130–132.

blessed souls on their thrones in the Mystic Rose of Paradise, St. Bernard addresses a prayer to the Virgin as symbol of Divine Grace to aid Dante, and he is permitted to have a glimpse of the great mystery of the Holy Trinity. He sees something that suggests the human image in the eternal light of the Godhead. If man is in God's image, there is something human to be discerned in the form divine.

IV. DANTE'S MYTHOLOGY

§ 38. *The Angelic Knowing*

ACCORDING to scholastic philosophy, the human mode of knowing differs from the angelic through this: the angels know by means of pure illumination, while men know by means of the symbolism involved in objects perceptible by the senses.[1] At first this seems a mere idle distinction based on no ascertained facts, and with a purely imaginary psychological distinction at its basis. But a careful consideration will discover an important thought in the definition.

It is readily granted that the growth of the human intellect is from particular facts to general truths. The immediate fact suggests to us presuppositions, and we learn to observe relations, and to think an object in its relations. Moreover, we discover correspondences between one series of phenomena and another, and thereby enrich our language by means of trope and metaphor. The poetic faculty of man thus arises. We especially learn to express our internal states and conditions

[1] *Paradiso*, xxix. 79–81.

— the feelings, desires, volitions, and ideas of the soul — by means of words that had originally only a material signification, and applied only to things perceptible by the senses.

So, too, our scientific activity has a movement from particular facts to general principles. At first there is a feeble effort at mere classification, or a statistical inventory. By and by laws are reached, and then energies are inferred as operating through these laws. Finally, knowledge becomes so complete that it sees principles, and in them recognizes energies acting in the form of laws. A natural principle is an energy or force or cause that acts according to its own laws, or, in other words, according to its definite nature.

When the scientific mind has reached a principle, it can deduce from it *a priori* the facts that will follow as results.

The application of science is called art. It is evident that the existence of art, properly so called, depends upon the possibility of guiding practice by a knowledge of principles.

In his philosophic activity, man traces back all principles to one principle as fundamental presupposition. From this one principle thus found, he descends by deduction along the line of principles, seeing the necessary causes and conditions that operate in the world, and comprehending the necessity of the general order and form of things and events.

Although man possesses and uses his capacity for philosophic knowledge, yet for the most part the activity of his mind is devoted to the inventory of particular facts and events, and to an equally special practical activity of arranging, ordering, and producing particular things and events, useful or hurtful to human interests.

If man should ever become so well acquainted with principles that he habitually put his knowledge into the form of deduction from the first principle, he would know by " pure illumination," just as the angels are said to know. To see at a glance the consequences of the energy of the first principle creatively descending from the universal toward the particular is to have pure illumination. But so long as one's knowledge of principles is so imperfect that he cannot comprehend them in the double sense of energy and law, he cannot use them deductively. In this respect human science is constantly on the road of progress. Some species of knowledge, like mathematics, have been deductive since the dawn of civilization.

Mathematical applications, like astronomy and other branches of physics, have long been deductive, and in a condition to predict results of combinations and processes. So, too, in the highest scientific minds in many departments of biology there are instances of men becoming so familiar with the principle of life in special provinces as to possess a ready intuitive knowledge which led them to numerous discoveries. They knew the whole from inspection of the part, because they had become so familiar with the analogies of nature that a luminous principle had come to be seen, and they could "anticipate experience," to use an expression of the philosopher Kant. Their intuition was a sort of "pure illumination," and, if they had been able to trace their principle back to the first principle so as to see vastly wider analogies, they would have attained to the veritable pure illumination which the schoolmen defined as the characteristic of angelic knowledge.

Human experience, therefore, is in the nature of a ladder which helps us to attain an elevation upon which we may walk securely without afterward needing the ladder. Of course I am aware that the empirical psychology of the present day does not take this view of the matter. It supposes that knowledge is firmly based on facts, and that it remains conditioned by them, and can never soar on its own wings without losing the certainty of scientific knowledge. But in this I conceive it has not followed its own advice and examined carefully the state of scientific knowledge, nor accurately analyzed the practical action of the scientific mind as it is actually employed in scientific questions. Rather than this, it furnishes us an example of what it condemns. It sweepingly concludes regarding the possibilities of knowledge and its necessary conditions, from supposed principles and supposed knowledge concerning the energy called mind and its laws of action.

But the poetic faculty of the soul, which we have already mentioned, is perhaps a more wonderful illustration of the distinction between the angelic and human modes of cognition, and of the ascent of the latter into the former. A great poet converts all things and events lying familiar about him in the world into tropes and similitudes, so that they lose their imposing airs of actuality, and become transparent images of ideas and spiritual truth. If he accomplishes so much as this by means of his tropes and personifications, he accomplishes far more than this by means of his entire poetic structures, for the individual tropes are only the brick and mortar of the poetic edifice. What the scientific principle is to the isolated facts and events, the poetic structure is to the separate tropes and personifications. It organizes them into a whole. It connects them with a central unity which stands to them in the twofold relation of efficient and final cause. It is at once their origin and the final purpose for which they exist.

§ 39. *The Poetic Mythus — What it Embodies*

It may be said that the supreme object of a great poetic work of art is the production of a myth. A myth furnishes a poetic explanation for a class of phenomena observed in the world. The mind that can see tropes in natural objects sees its way lighted by their converging rays to an underlying unity. Under tropes of small compass lie more extensive tropes, which unite the former into a consistent whole. And, as the poet's fundamental insight into the world is this, that the things and events of the world are means of spiritual expression, themselves moved and shaped by spiritual being, which they both hide and reveal, it follows that his combination of these poetic elements produces a whole structure that is spiritual throughout, and a revelation of human nature such as the poet has conceived and fitted to the world he has created.

Most beloved among mortal men is the poet. He is eyes to the blind and ears to the deaf. He is intuition and reflection for all. He furnishes his people a view of the world in which they can all unite. Hence he is the inspired Orpheus who builds cities and civilizations. His inspired mythus is recognized as the highest possession of the race, and implicit faith in it is demanded of all men. While it is permitted to deny the reality of existing facts and events, it is never permitted to deny the truth of the poetic mythus which unites a people in one civilization.

It is worth while, therefore, to study with all care the workings of a great poet's mind, and to note also what phases of nature he finds most available as vehicles for his myths. It has already been observed that the poet sees in the inanimate things and events of nature a revelation of rational will, — that is to say, of spiritual being like himself and humanity. Conscious being is the key to the universe in the poet's hands.

Not only in poetic art, but in all art, — sculpture, poetry, music, and architecture, — there is a seeking after rhythm, or after regularity, symmetry, and harmony, and a delight in them simply as such, as though they constituted indubitable evidence of a rational cause identical in nature with the human mind that beholds it. What is consciousness but the rhythm of subject and object continually distinguishing and continually recognizing and identifying? In this is regularity and symmetry, and also harmony. There is the repetition involved in self-knowing, — the self being subject and likewise object, — hence regularity. The shallowest mind, the child or the savage, delights in monotonous repetition, not possessing, however, the slightest insight into the cause of his delight. To us the phenomenon is intelligible. We see that his perception is like a spark under a heap of smoking flax. There is little fire of conscious insight, but much smoke of pleasurable feeling. He feels rather than perceives the fact of the identity which exists in form between the rhythm of his internal soul-activity and the sense-perception by which he perceives regularity.

§ 40. *The Sun Myth; its Significance as Physical Description of Mind*

The sun myth arises through the same feeling, illuminated by the poetic insight. Wherever there is repetition, especially in the form of revolution or return-to-itself, there comes this conscious or unconscious satisfaction at beholding it. Hence especially circular movement, or movement in cycles, is the most wonderful of all the phenomena beheld by primitive man. Nature presents to his observation infinite differences. Out of the confused mass he traces some forms of recurrence, — day and night, the phases of the moon, the seasons of the year, genus and species in animals and plants, the apparent revolutions of the fixed stars, and the orbits of planets. These phenomena furnish him symbols or types in which to express his ideas concerning the divine principle that he feels to be First Cause. To the materialistic student of sociology, all religions are mere transfigured sun myths. But to the deeper student of psychology it becomes clear that the sun myth itself rests on the perception of correspondence between regular cycles and the rhythm which characterizes the activity of self-consciousness. And self-consciousness is felt and seen to be a form of being not on a level with mere transient, individual existence, but the essential attribute of the Divine Being, Author of all.

Here we see how deep-seated and significant is this blind instinct or feeling which is gratified by the seeing and hearing of mere regularity. The words which express the divine in all languages root in this sense-perception and in the æsthetic pleasure attendant on it. Philology, discovering the sun-myth origin of religious expression, places the expression before the thing expressed, the symbol before the thing signified. It tells us that religions arise from a sort of disease in language which turns poetry into prose. But underneath the æsthetic feeling lies the perception of identity which makes possible the trope or metaphor.

In the poetic mythus there is a collection of those phenomena which have astonished the primitive consciousness of the race, and impressed on the soul a deep feeling of awe. Unutterable questions have made themselves dimly felt at the constant spectacle of nature's returning cycles. The activity of the mind with its regular and symmetrical recurrence or rhythm — the vibration between subject and object, its alternation of seizing an object at first new and unknown, and then recognizing (apperceiving) in it what is already become familiar, the alternation of subject and predicate — have not been recognized as the characteristics of mind, but these phenomena of return-into-self have excited its attention, and suggested first the far-off questions of the cycle of the soul reaching beyond this life into the hereafter.

Of all nations, the Egyptians were the most inclined to study these analogies of nature. Because of the fact that the supreme natural circumstance in Egyptian life is the Nile, and its cycles of rise and fall alternating with seed-time and harvest, this attention to cycles finds its natural occasion and explanation. The calendar and the signs of the seasons of the year became objects of the utmost solicitude. By and by the poetic faculty seized on the phenomena and the doctrine of immortality was embodied in a *mythus* for mankind. There is the still world of *Amenti* where the good Egyptian goes to dwell with Osiris.

But the most highly gifted of all peoples in

poetic insight were the Greeks. They possessed supreme ability in the interpretation of nature as expression of spirit.

They have countless mythuses to express the immortality of man and his after-life. Some of the more notable of these we must briefly consider.

§ 41. *Homer's Mythus of Hades*

In the eleventh book of Homer's "Odyssey" we have the Greek mythus of the state after death. The great poet Homer understands human freedom and retribution, making this circle of the deed and its return, however, include the gods on Olympus[1] and the life of men on earth in one process. He does not yet conceive the return of the deed as directly the affair of human society and the individual, and hence does not punish in his Hades the wickedness of men, although he symbolizes from a distance this species of retribution by the examples of Orion, Tityus, and especially of Tantalus and Sisyphus.

Orion is hunting beasts in the meadow of Asphodel. Tityus, the son of the very renowned

---

[1] Mr. D. J. Snider, in his essays on the *Iliad* (*Journal of Speculative Philosophy* for April and October, 1883; for January, July, and October, 1884; and for July, 1887), has shown clearly how this ethical process goes on, — one part of it on Olympus and the other part around Troy.

Earth, lies on the ground stretched over nine acres; two vultures gnaw his liver, and thus he expiates his violence done to Latona. Even Hercules, although delighted with banquets, is surrounded with a perpetual clang of the dead, and is continually startled and on the alert. He holds his naked bow and an arrow on the string, looking about terribly, always ready to let fly an arrow at some approaching monster. The atmosphere of earthly labors still envelops him.

"And I beheld Tantalus suffering severe griefs, standing in a lake; and it approached his chin. But he stood thirsting, and he could not get anything to drink; for as often as the old man stooped, desiring to drink, so often the water, being sucked up, was lost to him; and the black earth appeared around his feet, and the Deity dried it up. And lofty trees shed down fruit from the top, pear-trees, and apples, and pomegranates producing glorious fruit, and sweet figs, and flourishing olives; of which, when the old man raised himself up to pluck some with his hands, the wind kept casting them away to the dark clouds.

"And I beheld Sisyphus, having violent griefs, bearing an enormous stone with both his hands; he indeed, leaning with his hands and feet, kept thrusting the stone up to the top; but when it was about to pass over the summit, then strong force began to drive it back again; then the impudent stone rolled to the plain; but he, striving, kept thrusting it back, and the sweat flowed down from his limbs, and dust begrimed his head." [1]

It is interesting to note that Homer in his "Odyssey" first suggested the selection of Minos as judge in the lower world.

"There I beheld Minos, the illustrious son of Jove, having a golden sceptre, giving laws to the dead, sitting down, but the others around him, the king, pleaded their causes, sitting and standing through the wide-gated house of Pluto."

§ 42. *Plato's Threefold Future Life in the "Phædo"*

In Plato's "Phædo" we have a much more definite picture of the future state, involving not only the punishment of the wicked, but their purification also. To Plato, therefore, is to be accredited the invention of Purgatory and the discrimination of three states in the future life.

"For after death, as they say, the genius of each individual to whom he belonged in life leads him to a certain place in which the dead are gathered together for judgment, whence they go into the world below, following the guide who is appointed to conduct them from this world to the other; and when

[1] Buckley's Translation.

they have there received their due and remained their time, another guide brings them back again after many revolutions of ages. Now, this journey to the other world is not, as Æschylus says in the 'Telephus,' a single and straight path, — no guide would be wanted for that, and no one could miss a single path, — but there are many partings of the road, and windings, as I must infer from the rites and sacrifices which are offered to the Gods below, in places where three ways meet on earth. The wise and orderly soul is conscious of her situation and follows in the path; but the soul which desires the body, and which, as I was relating before, has long been fluttering about the lifeless frame and the world of sight, is, after many struggles and many sufferings, hardly and with violence carried away by her attendant genius, and when she arrives at the place where the other souls are gathered, if she be impure and have done impure deeds, or been concerned in foul murders or other crimes which are brothers of these, and the works of brothers in crime, — from that soul every one flees and turns away; no one will be her companion, no one her guide, but alone she wanders in extremity of evil until certain times are fulfilled, and when they are fulfilled she is borne irresistibly to her own fitting habitation, as every pure and just soul which has passed through life in the company and under the guidance of the gods has also her own proper home." [1]

Plato, too, gives a minute description of the Infernal rivers which Dante makes so impressive. He mentions Tartarus, Acheron, Pyriphlegethon, Styx, Cocytus, borrowing from Homer, who uses all of these,[2] as well as *Erebus*.

He then continues his account of the processes of punishment and purification: —

"Such is the nature of the other world; and when the dead arrive at the place to which the genius of each severally conveys them, first of all, they have sentence passed upon them, as they have lived well and piously or not. And those who appear to have lived neither well nor ill [or rather 'those who have lived average lives' (οἱ μέσως βεβιωκέναι); Professor Jowett's 'neither well nor ill' contradicts the 'evil deeds,' 'wrongs they have done to others,' and 'good deeds' spoken of below] go to the river Acheron and mount such conveyances as they can get, and are carried in them to the Acherusian lake; and there they dwell, and are purified of their evil deeds — [here is Purgatory] — and suffer the penalty of the wrongs which they have done to others, and are absolved, and receive

[1] *Phædo*, Jowett's Translation, p. 438.

[2] In the *Odyssey*, Book viii., except Tartarus, which occurs in the *Iliad*.

the rewards of their good deeds according to their deserts. But those who appear to be incurable by reason of the greatness of their crimes, — who have committed many and terrible deeds of sacrilege, murders foul and violent, or the like, — such are hurled into *Tartarus*, which is their suitable destiny, and they never come out [this is the Inferno]. Those, again, who have committed crimes which, although great, are not unpardonable, — who in a moment of anger, for example, have done violence to a father or a mother, and who have repented for the remainder of their lives, or have taken the life of another under the like extenuating circumstances, — these are plunged into Tartarus, the pains of which they are compelled to undergo for a year; but at the end of a year the wave casts them forth — mere homicides by way of Cocytus, parricides and matricides by Pyriphlegethon — and they are borne to the Acherusian lake, and there they lift up their voices and call upon the victims whom they have slain or wronged to have pity on them and to receive them, and to let them come out of the river into the lake. And if they prevail, then they come forth and cease from their troubles; but if not, they are carried back again into Tartarus, and from thence into the rivers unceasingly, until they obtain mercy from those whom they have wronged: for that is the sentence inflicted upon them by their judges. [Here we have Purgatory again, with the method of purification specified.] Those also who are remarkable for having led holy lives are released from this earthly prison and go to their pure home, which is above, and dwell in the purer earth; and those who have duly purified themselves with philosophy live henceforth altogether without the body in mansions fairer far than these, which may not be described [Plato's 'Paradiso'], and of which the time would fail me to tell."[1]

§ 43. *Plato's Mythus of Er. The Purgatory*

In the tenth book of his "Republic" Plato tells the story of Er, the son of Armenius, a Pamphylian, who was apparently slain on the field of battle, but had really fallen into a trance and remained thus until the twelfth day. On reviving, he told the story of his visit to the other world, where he beheld the last judgment. The just were sent upward on a heavenly way with a seal of judgment on their foreheads (suggesting Dante's seven *p's?*), while the unjust were commanded by the judges to "descend by the lower way on the left hand with the symbols of their deeds fastened on their backs." What is most wonderful in this story follows: For it seems that after judgment the souls go on jour-

[1] Jowett, 443, 444.

neys lasting a thousand years for each hundred years of their former lives (suggesting the period of the Procrastinators wandering on the lowest terrace). They come together, however, after the lapse of this period, both the good and the bad, and describe to each other their experiences, those who had gone below weeping and sorrowing at the recollection of their hard lot on their journey, and those who had gone above relating the delights and visions of beauty in heaven. After seven days of this reunion they set out anew on a journey to the place where they behold the spectacle of the universe with its eight heavens arranged like hollow shells around about the gigantic spindle of necessity that pierces through the universe as its axis of revolution. There is the outermost heaven (1) of the fixed stars, and then, arranged concentrically, the heavens of the planets, being as follows: (2) Saturn, next to the fixed stars; (3) Jupiter, second in whiteness; (4) Mars, reddish in hue; (5) Sun, brightest light; (6) Venus, whitest; (7) Mercury, like Saturn, both being yellowish; (8) Moon, colored by light reflected from the sun. Here is the suggestion of eight of Dante's heavens.

Each heaven moves at the song of a siren (Dante's Angels of the Hierarchy), and the music of all forms a harmony. Around about these heavens on the tripod of the universe sit the three fates, Lachesis singing of the past, Clotho of the present, and Atropos of the future. Clotho keeps in motion the heaven of the fixed stars, while Atropos guides the inner ones, giving them their various retrograde motions, and Lachesis assists at both. The journeying spirits, having arrived before Lachesis, now choose new lots of life, so that they may reascend to the earth. A prophet standing before Lachesis bids each choose his life freely, and in view of his experiences on the long journey he has undergone: " Your genius will not choose for you, but you will choose your genius. . . . Virtue is free, and, as a man honors or dishonors her, he will have more or less of her; the chooser is answerable, — God is justified."

Plato informs us that those who had experienced one human life before chose wiser than the new souls who had never before descended into bodies. The patterns of lives were spread out on the ground before the souls to choose from. Those who had reflected much and improved by experience, and " had acquired an adamantine faith in truth and right," were not dazzled by wealth and other allurements, but chose virtuous lives, and consequently happy ones. Others chose bad lives. The great idea of responsibility is emphasized in the strongest manner in this myth of Plato. It had not yet been born in the minds of the Greek people (witness the Nemesis that repressed high aspiration, — too much choice), and consequently we do not find it in the Greek religion. What we find in the Greek philosophy, however, gets realized in the mythus of succeeding ages. Note particularly in the myth of Er that it is the purgatorial idea that is uppermost. The present life is a probation, and the next life is determined at first by the present life. After a journey ten times the length of the present life, and the life determined by the present life, has passed away, a new life is to be chosen by the individual, with opportunity to avail himself of all his earthly experience as well as his experience in Hades. But Plato introduces the genuine Inferno for the worst species of tyrants and murderers, punishing treachery and violence by depriving the sinner of the privilege of journeying and of profitable experience in Hades. There are frames of mind, saw Plato, in which the individual does not profit by his experience, and such dispositions are hopeless; they are in the Inferno and not in the Purgatory.

Er relates that Ardiæus the Great (tyrant and parricide of Pamphylia) and other like sinners, attempting to come out of the "lower way" to the place of new choice, were seized and carried off by wild men of fiery aspect (Dante's demons of the

" Inferno "), who " bound them head, foot, and hand, and threw them down and flayed them with scourges, and dragged them along the road at the side, carding them on thorns like wool, and declaring to the pilgrims as they passed what were their crimes, and that they were being taken away to be cast into Tartarus."[1]

The state of mind of those who chose the worst lots is well depicted by Plato. One chooses a life of the greatest tyranny. " His mind having been darkened by folly and sensuality, he did not well consider, and therefore did not see at first that he was fated, among other evils, to devour his own children. But when he came to himself and saw what was in his lot, he began to beat his breast and lament over his choice, forgetting the warning of the prophet. For, instead of blaming himself as the author of his calamity, he accused chance and the gods, and everything rather than himself." This thought is adopted by Dante, we have seen, as a definition of the pervading frame of mind of the sinners in the " Inferno." " They blasphemed God and their parents; the human kind; the place, the time, and the origin of their seed and of their birth."[2]

Finally, when the souls had all chosen their lots in life they came to the Fates, who spun their

[1] Jowett.   [2] *Inferno*, iii. 103.

threads and made them irreversible; external circumstance has no power to change the resolution of the free will. "They then marched on in a scorching heat to the plain of forgetfulness, — λήθη (Dante's *Lethe*), — which was a barren waste destitute of trees and verdure, and toward evening they encamped by the river of Negligence (ἀμέλητα, lack of care or concern, general apathy, and loss of interest), the water of which river no vessel can hold." Plato makes Lethe a plain, while Dante makes it a river, following Virgil. Lack of interest is so near non-existence of character that no vessel can hold it. Not only the memory of the past is gone, but even all instincts and impulses, "organic memory," — all "karma," so to speak. "All were obliged to drink of this water, and those who were not saved by wisdom drank more than was necessary, and those who drank forgot all things. Now, after they had gone to rest, about the middle of the night, there was a thunder-storm and an earthquake, and suddenly they were all exploded, so to speak, like shooting stars, into the earthly life, and were born again as infants."

§ 44. *Virgil's Æneid. Descent of Æneas to Orcus*

In the sixth book of Virgil's Æneid there is another statement of the idea of the future life. It is full of hints which Dante has followed, but it is hardly an advance on the Platonic statement.

We might expect the Roman mind, especially given to the invention of legal forms and to the definition of the just compass of the human will with reference both to political and civil freedom, — *i. e.* freedom of life, limb, and property, and freedom by means of the latter from thraldom to nature, — we might expect that Virgil, a Roman, would give us a much more concrete and developed view of the idea of retribution in the future life. We are not altogether disappointed in this expectation, although we are compelled to notice that even Virgil is far from realizing in his poetic mind the mythus of the completely independent personal will, — the doctrine of perfect responsibility: he retains the doctrine of metempsychosis.

Æneas finds Charon the ferryman and the infernal rivers; he sees vast "prisons enclosed with a triple wall which Tartarean Phlegethon's rapid flood environs with torrents of flame, and whirls roaring rocks along. Fronting is a huge gate with columns of solid adamant, that no strength of men nor the gods themselves can with steel demolish. An iron tower rises aloft, and there wakeful Tisiphone sits watching." Here is evidently the suggestion of Dante's towers of the city of Dis, with its walls of iron heated to redness and guarded by the three furies. Cretan Rhadamanthus presides over this special realm of punishment of fraud, the furies being the ministers of justice. Below this extends Tartarus, wherein the Titan brood are punished. Again Dante has taken a hint for his lowest hell, making the giants encompass the pit of treachery. Treachery seeks the complete dissolution of all institutions. The giants even in Homer's "Odyssey" have this typical meaning. They do not live in villages, but isolatedly. Ulysses relates: "There are no assemblies for consultation among this people (the Cyclops), and they have no established laws. They live on mountain summits in hollow caves, each gives the law to his own family, and no one cares for his neighbors." They have no arts and trades, no commerce, no civilization.

Æneas next comes to the walls of Plato's realm and finds the Paradise of Trojan heroes, — "regions of joy, delightful green retreats and blessed abodes in groves, where happiness abounds." Here are found those who died fighting for their country, also "priests who preserved themselves pure and holy while life remained; pious poets who sang in strains worthy of Apollo; those who improved life by the invention of arts, and, in general, those who by worthy deeds have caused posterity to remember them."

On inquiring for Anchises, Musæus replies: "None of us have a fixed abode; in shady groves we dwell, or lie on couches all along the banks on meadows fresh with rivulets," etc. This suggests Dante's thought, that each of the souls in the "Paradiso" belongs to all the heavens, although they appear in special heavens to him. The interview with Anchises suggests that with Cacciaguida.[1]

Here, also, Æneas learns the doctrine of purgatory: —

"Meanwhile Æneas sees in the retired vale a grove situate by itself, shrubs rustling in the woods, and the river Lethe, which glides by those peaceful dwellings. Around this, unnumbered tribes and nations of ghosts were fluttering; as in meadows on a serene summer's day, when the bees sit on the various blossoms and swarm around the snow-white lilies, all the plain buzzes with their humming noise."

"These souls, for whom other bodies are destined by Fate, at the stream of Lethe's flood quaff care-expelling draughts and lasting oblivion."

"The spirit within (*spiritus intus alit*) nourishes the heavens, the earth, and watery plains, the moon, the sun, and the stars. The mind diffused through the limbs makes active the entire mass (*mens agitat molem*), and permeates the vast body

[1] *Paradiso*, xv., xvi., xvii.

of nature." This is the reason why the animals and man arise into existence.

"This fiery spiritual principle is of celestial origin, but souls are clogged by the influence of the body which is hurtful to spirit; material limbs and mortal bodies dull the powers of the soul.

"Hence they fear and desire, grieve and rejoice; and, shut up in darkness and a gloomy prison [the body], lose sight of their native skies. Even when with the last beams of light their life is gone, yet not every ill, nor all corporeal stains, are quite removed from the unhappy beings; and it is absolutely necessary [*i. e.* it cannot be but] that many imperfections which have long been joined to the soul should be in marvelous ways increased and riveted therein [*i. e.* should have become firmly fixed or ingrafted in the soul, — *inolescere*]. Therefore [because these stains should be removed] are they afflicted with punishments and pay the penalties of their former ills. Some, hung on high, are spread out to the empty winds [the purification by air, the second element above the earthy]; in others the guilt not done away is washed out in a vast watery abyss [the first element above the earthy], or burned away in fire [purification by the third element above the earthy]. We each endure his own manes [*i. e.* suffer for our sins, or 'Karma,' as the Hindoos call it; or, if 'manes' refers to Plato's 'genius,' — δαίμων, — then it means here the punishers or avengers]. Thence are we conveyed along [*i. e.* into] the spacious Elysium, and we, the happy few, possess the fields of bliss, till length of time, after the fixed period is elapsed, hath done away the inherent stain, and hath left the pure celestial reason and the fiery energy of the simple spirit [*i. e.* left it free from its stains]. All these [souls], after a thousand years have rolled away, are summoned forth by the God in a great body to the river Lethe; to the intent that, losing memory of the past, they may revisit the vaulted realms above [*i. e.* revisit the surface of the earth], and willingly return into bodies." [1]

§ 45. *Metempsychosis versus Eternal Punishment in Hell*

Metempsychosis — the doctrine of the transmigration of souls, or the return to earth of the soul after death and its reincarnation — we see is held by Plato and Virgil. This, too, although Plato makes the soul responsible for its choice of the lot in life that it shall lead.

It was necessary that Christianity should recognize the perfect responsibility of the human soul as well as its immortal destination. The mythus which

[1] Bohn's Translation, with emendations.

should contain the idea of complete freedom of the will, or, what is the same thing, perfected individuality, would be forced to express this insight by laying infinite stress on the determining power of the individual in this life. Nothing else could bring men to realize the true dignity of the human soul and its exalted destiny. The individual soul is strictly responsible to God and to the visible body of the Divine Spirit here on earth — the Church — for his choice of his career and for his deeds.

The only form in which the due emphasis could be given to this doctrine of responsibility was that chosen by the mythos of Hell — " bitter, remorseless, endless Hell " — as the future lot of all who reject the proffered eternal life, and refuse to enter the body of the Holy Spirit through union with the visible Church.

In translating the philosophical idea of essential or substantial into the poetic form of a mythus, it is always necessary to represent it by infinite time. The will, in determining itself, affects itself for all time. It determines itself completely in this life, and there is no probation in the next. This dogma alone could bring man to a consciousness of his independent personality, — his " substantia separata." In this way the mythus expressed the true and profound doctrine of the determinability of human destiny by the actual exertion of volition on the part of the soul itself, and of the utter non-effectiveness of vague postponement and reliance on external influences. External influences cannot initiate one's salvation, either here or hereafter: this is the doctrine of responsibility. The initiation lies always in free choice.

There is found no hope on the line of mortal sin, — only alienation more and more profound. It is not a progress; sin is not a necessary stage on the way to growth, but a retrogradation. Nevertheless, it is not extinction, — one can never reach that. Once immortality is reached, the individual remains a responsible being to all eternity. The negative will of the sinner builds up a wall of fate about him, it is true, but within this wall he ever holds his free volition, his absolute individuality.

Dante's poetic treatment of this mythus forms one of the few great works of all time.

§ 46. *Dante's Mythus of the Formation of the Inferno and the Purgatorial Mount*

Dante conceives that certain of the angels fell immediately after creation.[1] Before one could so much as count twenty, Lucifer fell. He struck the earth under Jerusalem and hollowed it out to the very centre, thus making the funnel-shaped Inferno,

[1] *Paradiso*, xxix. 47.

and raising on the opposite side in the southern Atlantic Ocean the mountain of Purgatory.

"On this side fell he down from heaven; and here the land, which erst stood out, through fear of him veiled itself with sea and came to our hemisphere; and perhaps, in order to escape from him, that which on this side appears, left here the empty space and upward rushed." [1]

The Mountain of Purgatory arises in the southern Atlantic Ocean; for the earth, according to his view, is not 8,000 miles in diameter, but only 6,500.[2] In the Southern Hemisphere Dante knows the most remarkable constellation of stars there. He probably had traveled far enough south to see them with his own eyes. He knows, too, the Precession of Equinoxes by which the pole of the heavens changes so as to bring up the Southern Cross to the view of Europeans: "Seen only by the primitive peoples," says he.

The streams of sorrow, wrath, malice, fraud, and treachery that flow down into this region Dante explains as flowing from the tears of the human race, which he figures as a gigantic Man standing within the Idæan mountain of Crete, and looking toward Rome. He borrows the external form of

[1] Carlyle, *Inferno*, xxx. 121.

[2] See, for some of the passages in which Dante gives this item, *Convito*, ii. 7; iii. 5.

the figure from the vision of the Great Image in Daniel, which there prefigured the fate of the Babylonian Empire and the world-movement of nations that followed it, — the rise of the Persian Empire under Cyrus, and possibly the final supremacy of Rome.

Daniel describes the King's dream: "This image's head was of fine gold, his breast and his arms of silver, his belly and his thighs of brass, his legs of iron, his feet part of iron and part of clay. . . . This head of gold is Nebuchadnezzar.

"And after thee shall arise *another kingdom* inferior to thee, and another *third kingdom* of brass, which shall bear rule over all the earth.

"And the *fourth kingdom* shall be as strong as iron; forasmuch as iron breaketh in pieces and subdueth all things, and as iron that breaketh all these, shall it break in pieces and bruise.

"And whereas thou sawest the feet and toes, part of potter's clay and part of iron, the kingdom shall be divided; but there shall be in it of the strength of the iron, forasmuch as thou sawest the iron mixed with miry clay. . . .

"And in the days of these kings shall the God of Heaven set up a kingdom which shall never be destroyed; and the kingdom shall not be left to other people, but it shall break in pieces and consume all these kingdoms, and it shall stand forever." . . .

Dante would think of the Roman Empire and the Christian Church as signified by this kingdom, which shall break in pieces all other kingdoms, but which shall itself stand forever. The Holy Roman Empire is, as we know, to Dante this kingdom. It was a stone carved out of a mountain, and it came to fill the whole earth, which clearly enough the Persian Empire never did, for it failed to conquer Europe.

§ 47. *Dante's Mythus of the Roman Empire*

Under the guidance of Virgil's mythus of the Roman Empire, Dante had been in the habit of looking upon Troy and the Trojans as the ancestors of the Romans. Crete, too, was a still more remote ancestor, — the nursery of Zeus, the god of civil order and the father of Minos, the first king who made just laws, and secured peace and harmony by their rigid execution.

Hence, too, Dante, in the "Inferno," shows so much bitterness toward the Greek heroes and statesmen, punishing, for example, Alexander and Pyrrhus in the seething purple flood of Phlegethon; Diomede and the great Ulysses in the *bolge* of evil counselors in the circle of fraud.

In the fourteenth canto of the "Inferno" Dante explains the origin of the rivers by this mythus of Crete and the Image of the Human Race, or perhaps, more accurately, the Image of Human Civil Government (as the reference to Daniel's vision seems to indicate): —

"'In the middle of the sea lies a waste country,' he then said, 'which is named Crete,'[1] under whose King the world once was chaste. A mountain is there, called Ida, which once was glad with waters and foliage; now it is deserted like an antiquated thing. Rhea of old chose it for the faithful cradle of her son; and, the better to conceal him when he wept, caused cries to be made on it.

"Within the mountain stands erect a great Old Man, who keeps his shoulders turned toward Damietta, and looks at Rome as if it were his mirror. His head is shapen of fine gold, his arms and his breast are pure silver; then he is of brass to the cleft; from thence downward he is all of chosen iron, save that the right foot is of baked clay, and he rests more on this than on the other. Every part, except the gold, is broken with a fissure that drops tears, which collected perforate that grotto. Their course descends from rock to rock into this valley. They form Acheron, Styx, and Phlege-

---

[1] Virgil, *Æneid*, iii. 104: —

"Creta Jovis magni medio jacet insula ponto
Mons Idæus ubi, et gentis cunabula nostræ;
Centum urbes habitant magnas, uberrima regna
Maximus unde pater, si rite audita recordor
Teucrus Rhœteas primum est advectus in oras."

thon; then, by this narrow conduit, go down to where there is no more descent. They form Cocytus; and thou shalt see what kind of lake that is; here, therefore, I describe it not."[1]

In Virgil[2] we find the suggestion which reveals to us the idea in Dante's mind in its entirety: "Crete, the island of great Jove, lies in the middle of the sea, where is Mount Ida and the nursery of our race; they inhabit a hundred great cities, most fertile realms, whence Teucer, our first ancestor, if rightly I remember the things I have heard, was first carried to the Rhœtian coasts [promontory of Troas], and there selected the place for his kingdom. Ilium stood not yet," etc.

According to Apollodorus,[3] Teutamus, the son of Dorus and a descendant of Deucalion, mythic founder of the Dorian race, came to Crete with a Greek colony. In the time of his son Asterion, Zeus came to Crete with Europa and became father of Minos, Sarpedon, and Rhadamanthus, who were adopted by Asterion upon his marriage with Europa.

Zeus, according to the Greek mythus, is the divine founder of civil order, and to be son of Zeus is to be a hero of civilization. Minos became the greatest king of the mythic heroic period, being

[1] Carlyle, *Inferno*, xiv. 94–120.   [2] *Æneid*, iii. 104.
[3] iii. 1, § 1.

the inventor of wonderful laws for the securing of justice. He freed the seas of pirates.

The circumstances of his obtaining his kingdom gave rise to feuds symbolized by the story of the wild bull of Crete, — probably an independent freebooter who sought alliance with Minos. The Minotaur is the symbol of blood violence which Minos repressed by shutting up the monster in a labyrinth wonderfully constructed.

§ 48. *The Minotaur and the Labyrinth in the Light of this Mythus*

In the myth of the labyrinth we have a symbolic description of the nature of feuds and blood violence, and of the manner in which they are suppressed by a Jove-nurtured king. Within a labyrinth, the avenues continually lead from one into the other without making any progress toward a final goal. One goes forward and forward, but after weary labors finds himself at length where he started, or even farther off from his goal.

So long as there was no kingly authority and no just laws, feuds arose; violence on the part of one led to retaliation on the part of another, and this to counter retaliation. Each avenging of a deed was taken as a new case of violence to be avenged again.

Thus the island of Crete and the surrounding

nations were in a labyrinth of blood revenge. The Minotaur is used by Dante as symbol of blood revenge; and the labyrinth, which is not named in the "Divina Commedia," signifies the endless nature of feuds thus avenged.

But the labyrinth has also the meaning of a code of justice which imprisons the Minotaur; for when this system of blood revenge is throttled by just laws, the state steps in, and, apprehending the first aggressor, makes a labyrinth of him by making his deed return upon him at once, and thus rendering unnecessary the blood revenge on the part of the injured one; hence the labyrinth in this sense is a device by which the endless progress of private revenge is stopped in its first steps,—it is shut up, and the labyrinth is reduced to a jail or prison conducted according to just criminal laws. Formerly all Crete was a labyrinth, and all the neighboring islands of the Ægean seas and the mainland were infested by pirates and robber states continually at feud with each other. Minos, it is said, not only checked piracy about Crete, but made himself master of the Greek islands, and was able, it seems, to punish the blood violence and treachery even of a colony like Athens. His son Androgeus was assassinated at Athens on account of some jealousy or feud. Minos subdued Megara, and compelled the Athenians to send every nine years or oftener a tribute of fourteen youths and maidens to be devoured by the Minotaur, — that is to say, confined in the labyrinth as hostages, or perhaps executed for new deeds of violence done against Cretans.

It was the national hero of Athens, Theseus, also a law-giver, who slew this Minotaur, at least so far as the Athenian tribute was concerned, — probably entering into a treaty by which he suppressed the blood violence of his own subjects and assisted Minos in his endeavors to suppress such violence everywhere, and thus put an end to the Minotaur altogether.

Wonderful insight, therefore, Dante displays in making the Minotaur or blood violence stand as guardian at the entrance of the circles of violence.

From this good law-maker, Minos, descends the Trojan Æneas, as Virgil asserts and Dante believes, and hence by direct descent the Roman Empire, appointed by divine right to give laws to the whole world and suppress the complex of private revenge and feuds, — a complex in the fact that each avenging deed is a new crime, and thus forms a labyrinth out of which it is impossible to extricate the state. Dante knew — bitterly knew — how this labyrinth of blood revenge extended over his native Italy; cities divided by factions and continually at war with each other.

§ 49. *Minos as Judge in the Light of this Mythus*

The island of Crete has great significance to Dante for these reasons: He accordingly selects Minos, as the typical dispenser of justice, to preside over the court of the Inferno, following Homer and Virgil in this choice. Minos invented a code which secured the return of his own deed, or at least its symbol, upon the criminal. The sinners, on entering the presence of Minos, lay open their secret lives to him. His judgment is indicated by coiling about him his tail, "making as many circles round himself as the number of grades or circles that the sinner will have to descend." Minos symbolically indicates that the sinner's own bestiality has made its coil about him, and that the sinner's own deed makes his circle of hell.

§ 50. *Other Mythologic Figures used by Dante*

It is noteworthy that Virgil places in the gates of his Inferno Centaurs, Briareus, the Chimæra, the Lernæan Hydra, Harpies, and the three-bodied Geryon — all indicating the instrumentalities that send men to their death. Dante uses most of these figures in his own way, always showing a profound insight into the capacity of the symbol for spiritual expression.

The Centaurs were nomadic peoples, without

organized laws of justice, who marauded on the Greek civil communities, and escaped punishment on their swift horses; hence also they are symbols of violence of a special kind. Dante employs them to guard the banks of Phlegethon and punish the violent. It is the fitting punishment of the violent that they make for themselves an environment of violence. The Centaurs were also teachers of the Greek heroes in the arts of single combat, medicine, and music, — means useful to a life of roving adventure, — but they were not teachers of laws; of the art of commanding armies or organized bodies; of anything specially useful to cities. Like the Cyclops, they symbolize man as individual apart from man as social whole, — the little self over against the greater self.

The Harpies are placed by Dante in the doleful woods of the suicides as symbolic of their hypochondria. The gloomy presage of coming evil causes suicide. These are birds, airy creatures, symbolic therefore of fancy and the future. They defile the feast of the present with forebodings of evil.

The Furies and the Gorgons guard the sixth circle, from of old the symbols of all that is destructive in violence against civil order, — discord, slander, mistrust, suspicion, and deadly revenge. Medusa the Gorgon paralyzes the beholder: is it hardened rebellion against God (as Carlyle thinks), is it atheism or petrifying skepticism regarding immortality (as Philalethes thinks), or is it simply panic terror which deprives one of all control of his limbs? — a significance which the Greeks may have given to the Medusa face. One may see the reflection of such panic fear, — *i. e.*, hear of it at a distance, — but he must not look upon it directly if he would escape its paralyzing effects.

Geryon is the well-described image of fraud in Dante's portraiture. The ancients did not thus specially characterize him. He was simply the three-bodied king of Hesperia, who owned the famous herd of oxen that Hercules obtained. Perhaps Dante confounded him with Cacus, the wily thief of the oxen in Virgil's story. He is represented with the face of the just man, mild of aspect. The fraudulent purpose is covered with a special appearance of conformity to law and justice, — submission of the individual will to the general will of the community. But he has a reptile's body covered with knots and circlets like a lizard or a toad, the paws of a beast, and an envenomed scorpion tail. He seeks not, like the violent, to rob his fellow-men directly, and attack the civil order with his individual might. But he seeks to use the civil order against itself, under a semblance of obedience to it, to gain the faith of men and then abuse their confidence. This, of course, will weaken their reliance on civil order. While direct violence forces every one to trust civil order all the more, and draw close to the protecting shelter of the state, Fraud, on the other hand, weakens the faith of the citizen in the power of the state to protect him. For, see, have not I been wronged under the semblance of mild-faced Justice?

The Giants in the lowest round have already been mentioned as typical of the entirely savage state of society, utterly isolated human life. The individual by himself must do all for himself. He cannot share with others the conquest of nature. It is his own individual might against the world. The subduing of wild beasts, the cultivation of the soil, the arts of manufacture, — in all these he is unaided. Worse than all, he is deprived of human intercourse, and does not inherit the accumulated wisdom and experience of the human race. Homer, as we saw, has painted this state of savagery in the Cyclops.

Cerberus furnishes a familiar type of greed in general. Dante, after Virgil, makes him the type of intemperance and gluttony.

Plutus, the ancient god of wealth, presides over the fourth circle of the " Inferno." The avaricious make property their god; it should be their means for achieving earthly freedom and leisure for divine works such as tend to the spiritual good of one's fellow-men, and one's own growth in wisdom. The prodigal misuse their property, and are always in want, or "hard up," as the slang phrase has it. Hence they are always trying to come at a little money to help them over a "tight place." Hence, too, they are always giving their minds to getting property, and are in the same hell with the avaricious. Both long for property in the same degree.

Charon, the infernal ferryman, is likewise borrowed from Virgil, and is not found in the early Greek poets. His fiery eyes and wheels of flame, — typical of the red-weeping eyes of mourners for the dead, or possibly a symbol of his keen watchfulness required to separate (in Virgil's "Inferno") the souls whose bodies are buried with due ceremony from those unsepultured, or, in Dante's "Inferno," to exclude the souls of the pusillanimous from his boat, — this circumstance of the flaming eyes is also borrowed from Virgil.

§ 51. *The Mythus of Dante's " Purgatorio"*

The finest portion of the "Divina Commedia" is unquestionably the Purgatory, but it needs the "Inferno" to precede it for the sake of effect. It is filled with the light of the stars, the verdure of spring, growth of character, and the aspiration for perfection. In it the human will shows its true power to make the years reinforce the days; while in the "Inferno" there is constant self-contradiction of the will, and constant building-up of Fate between man and society.

The mythus of Purgatory is more entirely Dante's work than that of the "Inferno." He found it a shadowy middle state of the soul, and built it up into a systematic structure, definitely outlined in all its phases. It is *the* true state of man as a condition of perpetual education in holiness here and hereafter. All men who are struggling here in the world with an earnest aspiration for spiritual growth can find no book to compare with the second part of Dante's Poem. In climbing the steep sides of this mountain, the air continually grows purer, and the view wider and less obstructed. On the summit is the terrestrial paradise of the Church, symbolizing the invisible Church of all sincere laborers for good on earth. The Church on earth holds humanity in so far as it lives in the contemplation of the divine, and in the process of realizing the divine nature in the will and in the heart. Dante collects in a complex symbol the various ceremonial devices of the Church, — almost mechanically, in fact. It is an allegory rather than a poetic symbol. But he adds dramatic action to it, first by introducing the scene between Dante and

Beatrice, secondly by the dumb show of the history of the Church, — the tragedy of its corruption, its seizure by France, and its transfer from Rome to Avignon.

§ 52. *The Mythus of Dante's "Paradiso" — Gnosticism*

The mythus of the "Paradiso" is constructed on a wholly new plan. There is no hint of it elsewhere except in the Platonic myth in the "Phædo" (the allusion to the complete disembodiment of the soul). The Mysticism of sixteen hundred years enters it as material.

Gnosticism represented the first attempt to reconcile Christianity with philosophy, as Neoplatonism represented a later attempt on the part of Greek Philosophy to reach the Oriental unity by transcending the first principle of Plato and Aristotle.

Gnosticism and Neoplatonism, accordingly, have substantially the same problem before them. Both systems agree in adopting the doctrine of Philo that God is exalted above virtue and knowledge, and even above good and evil together. Plato had identified God with the Absolute Good, while Aristotle had made him Absolute Reason.

From God, according to Gnosticism and Neoplatonism, there emanates Nous as his image, and then, directly or after some interval, the Psyche or Soul, from which emanates finally matter or body from the soul as the soul's object, created result, or achievement.

These four cardinal points are common to all Gnostic and Neoplatonist systems; but great diversity exists in regard to intermediate steps, and in regard to names and definitions. Gnosticism likes to use the word "æon" (αἰών) where Platonism likes the word "idea." By æon it means individual or complete cycle of activity, — a self-determined being (*substantia separata*), in short. There may be many ideas or æons, or complete cycles of process, between the Nous or Reason and the Soul. There are, in fact, twenty-eight of these in the system of Valentinus (who came to Rome from Alexandria about the year 140 A. D.). He made thirty æons in all, — wishing to symbolize the thirty years of Christ's life, as is said, somewhat as Dante wished to do this by the number thirty-three (the number of the cantos in each part of the "Divina Commedia"). These æons were yoked together in pairs, each pair being called a syzygy, — such a syzygy being, for example: 1. Truth (ἀλήθεια). +2. Reason (Νοῦς). These beget the second syzygy. 3. The creative word (λόγος). +4. Life (ζωή). The Word and Life beget the third syzygy. 5. Man (ἄνθρωπος). +6. Church (ἐκκλησία), and so on until one comes to Sophia (Σοφία) or wisdom, which is the youngest of the third division of æons, and (we are curious to learn) is conscious of her remoteness from God, and hence flies toward God, the source of emanation. Wisdom proceeds to imitate the other æons by creating, but begets only chaos and confusion. In her grief at this dreadful result, the other æons take pity and conspire with God to produce two new æons, — Christ and the Holy Spirit, — who redeem the world of chaos and confusion, acting as the Demiurgos, or world-builder. Here we have a mythus of the fall into finitude, — the lapse from the One to the Many, from the Perfect to the Imperfect, and the redemption from the latter.

In Proclus's system there are many unities issuing from the primal essence, — all above life and reason and the power of comprehension. Then there are many triads corresponding to æons between reason and matter. Marcion of Pontus had no æons in his system of Gnosticism, but retained the Demiurgos, or world-maker (as Jehovah of the Old Testament, who is opposed to Christ as Saviour).

The emanation theories of both Gnosticism and Neoplatonism have the principle of Lapse as the principle of their philosophic method, and not the principle of self-determination, which is the true principle of philosophic method. The principle of Lapse finds only a descending scale, and is obliged to introduce an arbitrary and miraculous interference into its world-order, in order to explain progressive development and redemption. The principle of self-determination shows us an ascending scale, all of whose steps are miraculous, and yet none of them arbitrary.

In the later forms of Neoplatonism there is a slight trace of return toward the pure doctrines of Aristotle and Plato. The pupils of Plutarch of Athens seem to have learned from him that Plato and Aristotle substantially agree in their worldview. Syrianus and Hierocles, of Alexandria, the former the teacher of Proclus, both recognize this fact, and Hierocles insists that Ammonius Saccas, the founder of Neoplatonism, proved once for all the substantial agreement of the two great Greek philosophers. Proclus, in his great work on the theology of Plato, treating chiefly of the dialogue of "Parmenides," has undertaken, however, to show that Plato himself holds the doctrine of a primal essence above reason, in several of his works: such an essence would, of course, be unrevealed and unrevealable, and thus could not be the God of Christianity. Proclus lived a century and a half after Christianity had become the state religion; and the Neoplatonic school at Athens was closed in 529 by Justinian, forty-four years after the death of Proclus. The influence of the school continued into Christian philosophy and mysticism for many centuries, the chief channel through which this influence flowed being the writings of the Pseudo-Dionysius, about whom Dante readers hear so much.

§ 53. *The Mythus of the "Paradiso" developed in the Doctrine of the Celestial Hierarchies*

The chief work of Dionysius, according to historians, must have been written after the year 450, because it contains expressions used in the Council of Chalcedon in 451.[1] Purporting to be written by the first Bishop of Athens, a convert of St. Paul, the work exercised great authority. Its chief doctrine is that, of the fourfold division of natures

---

[1] The following is condensed from Ueberweg's account: "The writings that purport to be the works of Dionysius the Areopagite of Athens (Acts xvii. 34), first Bishop of Athens, are mentioned first in the year A. D. 532. They were accepted as genuine and of high authority on account of the connection of their supposed author with Paul. They gained credit in the Church in the eighth and ninth centuries, and after a commentary had been written on them by Maximus Confessor early in the seventh century. Laurentius Valla, about the middle of the fifteenth century, asserted their spuriousness, which was demonstrated afterward by Morinus, Dallæus, and others."

into (1) that which is created and does not create, — matter; (2) that which is created but creates again, as, for example, souls; (3) that which creates but is not created, as Christ, the Logos; and (4) that which neither creates nor is created, as the Absolute One, or the Father. Here is Neoplatonism in its most heretical form.

The highest cannot be called by a name, according to Dionysius. It may be spoken of symbolically only. It is above truth and above goodness; nor does it create.

Through the thinking of the Gnostics and Neoplatonists, using the results of Plato and Aristotle, and endeavoring to solve the problems of Christianity by them, arose a new *mythus*, — a mythus of symbolic thinking, which came over into Christian Theology as the doctrine of the Celestial Hierarchy. On this mythus Dante has constructed his "Paradiso." It is modified to meet the wants of Christian doctrine in such a manner that what were emanating Æons or Ideas become one hierarchy of Angels, consisting of nine separate orders, divided, according to office and participation in divine gifts, into three triads.

The highest triad behold God's judgments directly, and are called Thrones; but there are two grades of excellence above the common rank of these, — to wit, Cherubim, who are filled perfectly with divine light, and hence *comprehend* most. The Seraphs are filled more especially with divine charity, and excel in *will-power*. The common angels of this class are called Thrones.

The second triad are distinguished for announcing things divine, and are called Powers, the common principle of all being this. But elevated to an extraordinary degree are Dominions, who are supreme in ability to distinguish the proper order and fitness of what is to be done. Then, secondly, the Virtues, who are eminent in providing the faculty of fulfilling or in planning the means.

The lowest triad has the common function of arranging and executing the duties of the angelic ministry so far as it deals directly with men. Angels are the common principle, Archangels the superior, and Principalities the highest directors of this function of angelic ministry.

These bizarre expressions, used to name the different degrees of celestial perfection, arose in the interpretation of obscure passages in St. Paul's writings.

In Romans we have a passage speaking of "death, life, angels, principalities, powers, things present and things to come;" and a still more remarkable passage in Colossians:[1] "By him were all things created, that are in heaven, and that are

[1] i. 16, 17.

in earth, visible and invisible, whether they be thrones, or dominions, or principalities, or powers: all things were created by him, and for him: and he is before all things, and by him all things consist."

This passage is otherwise famous as the most important place in which St. Paul gives his version of St. John's doctrine of the Word, or Logos, which was in the beginning, and which made all created things.

§ 54. *The Heretical Tendency in this Mythus*

It is essential to note that the hierarchy may be interpreted to mean that the highest, or the Thrones (Seraphim, Cherubim, Thrones), are of an angelic ministry more removed from mediation with what is below, — more immediate in their contemplation of the divine. This is heretical when the mediation is denied, — *i. e.*, when it is thought to be more divine to be above and apart from the world of humanity; but not heresy, when it is held that "Thrones" *complete* their mediation perfectly, and come to use their power to elevate fallen humanity, and are not held aloof as through fear of contamination by contact with sinners. The Highest Logos goes down into the manger of Space and Time, and raises all up ; as contemplative Cherub, the Logos pierces clear through the mediation of time and space intellectually and philosophically, and sees the face of God. As Seraph, it loves God through loving all creation, down to the lowest insect or plant or clod.

Seraph and Cherub are of the highest triad, because they make the deepest and completest mediation, and see clearest the divine shining through creation. They can see the praise of God even in sin and evil. But the danger of heresy lurks in this doctrine. If it is held that the Cherubim see God directly face to face *without* the mediation of creation, then mere quietism is reached. Buddhism holds that the highest states of perfection for its saints are most aloof from the world of man and nature.

"From the lowest to the highest stations of human activity, to serve as a servant who does menial work is everywhere necessary. For the lowest class of laborers, whatever they do is only a trade; for the next higher it is an art; and for the highest, whatever they do is to them the image of the totality." (Paraphrase of one of Goethe's sayings.)

Hence it is not the angels, archangels, and principalities that make the human mediation most perfectly. It is to them a "trade." But the powers, virtues, and dominions are higher toward a perfect mediation, and can go down lower into the depths safely to bring up the lowest. But the thrones can make the complete mediation from lowest to highest.

Dante has connected this artificial system (which refuses, even in the expositions of its greatest disciples, to take on a perfectly rational and logical form) to the heavens of the Ptolemaic system, and thereby fastened his degrees of spiritual perfection to astronomical distinctions observable by all men. In the "Convito," Second Treatise, chapter xiv., he has stated in detail his astronomical theory.

That there remained a sediment of Neoplatonism, and hence of Oriental thinking, in Dante's mind, even after the chidings of Beatrice in the Terrestrial Paradise, and perhaps, too, even in the teachings of Beatrice herself in the twenty-eighth canto of the "Paradiso," may well be believed. But the main great points of his theology, founded on Aristotle as interpreted by the Schoolmen, will stand the scrutiny of all time.

The doctrine of the divine form, or the self-activity of the absolute, involves the common nature of man and God, or God as divine-human. This is the great central truth (of which the doctrine of the Trinity is the symbol) on which all modern civilization is built, and it is its open secret.

§ 55. *The Symbol of the Trinity embodies the Highest Philosophic Truth*

God, the absolute reason, is perfect knowing and willing in one — what he knows he creates; for his knowing causes to be that which he intellectually perceives. His intuition of himself, then, contemplates the eternal Word — the Second Person — equal in all respects to himself. The Second Person, the Logos, knows and wills likewise himself, and thus arises a Third Person. But a difference makes its appearance here: the Second Person knows himself as having been begotten, in the timeless past of "The Beginning," as having arisen through all stages of imperfection up to the highest. This knowledge is also creation, and the Word creates a world of imperfect beings in the form of evolution from pure space and time up to the highest and holiest on earth, — the "New Jerusalem," the "City of God," the "Invisible Church," whose spirit is the Holy Spirit, or the Third Person. The world of man and nature thus belongs to the *processio*, — to the hypostasis of derivation, or the genesis of the Eternal Word. The Logos, contemplating its own derivation, logically implied, causes it to be, as an actual creation in Time and Space. As the Holy Spirit proceeds from all eternity, it is not a generation, but a procession always complete, but always continuing. Here is the highest view possible of human nature; it is part of the procession of the Holy Spirit.

Man reaches perfection in the infinite, eternal, immortal, and invisible Church.

This is the River and the Great White Rose of Paradise.

The symbol of philosophy as the knowledge of the highest truth is Beatrice, and Dante has recorded his conviction that this highest truth is revealed and can be known in the following words:

"I see well that our intellect is never sated if the truth does not illuminate it, beyond whose circuit no truth exists. In that truth it reposes, as a wild animal in its lair, as soon as it has reached it. And it can reach it; for, were this not so, all desire would be created in vain."[1]

[1] *Paradiso*, iv. 124–129.

V. A SUMMARY

§ 56. *The Doctrine of Sin the Central Theme of the Divina Commedia*

In the eighteenth canto of his "Purgatorio," Dante lays down the doctrine of freedom, which is the basis of responsibility, and hence of that which makes sin and punishment possible.

"Every substantial form that is separate from matter, and yet is united with it, possesses a generic energy within itself which manifests itself only in its operations, and cannot be perceived except in its effects or in what it does." A substantial form is thus described as a self-active energy — a living being. God is such a substantial separate being; disembodied spirits or angels are held to be such; and, thirdly, human beings in the body fall in the same class. We cannot perceive true individualities by the senses. Seeing, hearing, tasting, smelling, and touching afford us knowledge only of physical or material forms, and those are all divisible and changeable and perishable. Not one of them is the principle that combines the material parts. We think of the life principle as a separate essence, which builds up the body and uses it for the manifestation of self-activity.

Dante goes on to say that man does not know the origin of his instinctive appetites nor of his primary ideas. They are to him part of his original possession. He finds himself with appetites and desires, and with logical forms of thinking, and with categories of thought or primitive ideas, that he cannot get rid of. He is not responsible for these because they are not his own conscious product, — he does not will his body, nor his instincts, nor his ideas. Then, next, there is free will, which considers and chooses and "holds the threshold of assent." What it is and does, it is responsible for, because it is the power of self-determination. The instincts and the primary ideas belong only to that generic energy which cannot be perceived except in its effects. But the free will stands in the doorway of action, and considers and chooses which it will realize. Whatever it chooses to do, that it adopts as its own, and is responsible for it. This principle of self-determination or free will, says Dante, is that to which merit attaches according as it collects and winnows out good and evil loves. The deep reasoners, who have searched the foundations, he continues, have seen this innate liberty in the soul, and accordingly have set up moral or ethical principles, and claimed their validity for the world. Human instincts or desires, that is, human love, therefore is by nature, and therefore of necessity, and man is not responsible for them. But the power of governing this love is, says Dante, in us. *Di ritener lo è in voi la potestate.* No matter what the gifts to man, — be they good or evil, — no matter what the environment be, or what its action on the human being, he is a separate subsistence, an independent being, an essence or individual selfhood apart from his environment. He is not responsible for these gifts or endowments, or for the action of his environment upon him, but responsible only for what he himself does with these gifts and with his environment. His reaction is his own.

In the previous canto (seventeenth of "Purgatorio"), Virgil is made to explain the whole doctrine of sin from this point of view. "Neither Creator nor created was ever without love, — instinctive love or rational love (*i. e.*, love for immediate objects of the senses, or love for objects perceptible only by thought, such as God, and human institutions and arts). Natural love," says Dante, " is always free from error. But the love that depends on reason may err through a bad object, or by excess, or by deficiency of vigor. If this love is directed towards a proper object (as, for example, toward God or virtue), it cannot be evil. Nor can it be evil when it is moderately directed towards the goods of this world, the enjoyment of the senses," — *i. e.*, when subordinated to the love for God and the good. "But when love turns aside to evil, or seeks the good with excess or defect, it operates against the Maker. Consequently, love in man may be the seed of every virtue, and likewise of every fault that deserves punishment."

"A being cannot hate itself." It may hate its deed, or its thought, but not itself. Dante says, too, that a being cannot really hate its first cause or Creator, because it cannot be conceived as standing apart from its first cause. But he cannot mean that the human soul is not independent enough from God to hate what he conceives to be the actions of God. Of course, in so far as an individual thinks God as his essence and as the substance of his selfhood, he must love God. In so far as he conceives God as hostile to his interests and desires, the sinner hates God. Dante goes on to explain that the sinner does not hate God, but rather his neighbor. He loves the evil that happens to his neighbor, and this love takes one of three forms. A man may have pride, and hope for happiness through the loss of his fellow-men, and wish to climb through their misfortunes, and profit by their injury.

Secondly, he may have envy, and fear to lose power, grace, honor, and fame in case some other person has good fortune in these respects. Hence he comes to love the contrary. There does not seem to be much difference between the first and the second kind of sin here mentioned by Dante. Both wish evil for the neighbor, and both wish good for the self at the expense of the neighbor.

The third kind of sin which loves evil for its neighbor is anger, which through injury appears to become gluttonous of vengeance.

These may be called the three sins of perverted love. But there is a love which is defective, and this is sloth. Then there is a love excessive ; as Dante says, " love which hastes to the good with order violated," incontinence, which has three forms, — avarice, intemperance, and lust.

These are the seven mortal or deadly sins, — deadly because they defeat the true ends of the soul, which are intellectual insight into nature and mind, unselfish love of man, and will-power industriously exercised in the world to realize the good, to lift up the fallen, to enlighten the ignorant and comfort the afflicted, and everywhere to help all people to help themselves.

These seven mortal sins, one and all, conflict with this high end of life, because they attack the necessary conditions of spiritual life, or, what is the same thing, they attack the foundations of civilization. Civilization is a vast process of mutual helpfulness secured among mankind. It is built up on four vast pillars called institutions, — the family, civil society, the state, and the church. Strike at these institutions, and the pillars of civilization are struck. Each one of these mortal sins attacks one or more of these pillars that support civilization, and endangers in some way the process of mutual helpfulness which makes human life superior to the life of the lower animals.

The lowest and most deadly of these mortal sins, for example, is directed against all social union of man with men; not merely against the fruits that follow from social union, but against its very essence. It refuses to associate. Pride aims to isolate itself from the universe. It wishes to be all-sufficient for itself. Its fruits are treachery in the family, in society, in the state, and in the church. Its blows are aimed directly against the existence of the social bond, and in so far forth as its deeds are effective, it freezes up the kindly relations between man and men, and the result is symbolized by the frozen lake of Cocytus.

Envy is the next sin; it is not so deadly as pride, because it feels more interest in the acts and deeds of its fellow-men. It desires to share in the productions of its fellow-men; it wishes the material goods and the spiritual goods of its fellows, but it desires them at the expense of depriving others of them. Envy goads the soul to commit sins of fraud. In this it, too, like pride, strikes against the social tie that binds society together. For by deceit — using the forms of justice in order to cheat one's neighbors of their just dues — one undermines the respect which ought to exist for the forms of justice. Anger strikes at individuals by violence, and does not attack the forms of society, as envy does, by using fraud. Envy strikes against the institution of property, rendering it insecure by thefts and briberies, forgery and counterfeiting. It destroys the trust of men in the means invented by the race to secure our freedom from the wants of food, clothing, and shelter. Envy attacks personal character and its safeguards by hypocrisy, flattery, fraudulent impersonation, evil counsel, and schism, making each man distrustful of his fellows. But it does not isolate man so deeply as pride. Pride tends to sever all social intercourse, while envy desires only to reap the fruits of social life, but at the expense of society itself. Envy wishes the good of men but through their loss. Pride wishes no share either in society, or in its fruits. Anger produces these evils in a less degree, because it is special in its effects. It is directed against this or that particular person, and instead of undermining our respect for law, it causes us to appreciate all the more the service of well-established law in protecting us from violence.

Sloth attacks the institutions of civilization by

paralyzing the will. It undermines the industry which conquers nature and educates the mind.

Avarice and waste injure society by diverting property from its place as means of realizing human freedom. The social interchange by which the individual is enabled to contribute something of his own deeds for the benefit of his fellow-men, and to draw out in his turn from the market of the world his share of the aggregate of productions, is rendered possible by means of the institution of private property. There could be no transfer of the individual will to the social whole, unless the individual were permitted to impress his will on things and make them his property. Consequently, without the institution of private property he could not help society, and this would render impossible on the other hand his participation in the labor of the race; he could receive nothing from his fellow-men because nothing could be collected or transmitted. Hence the significance of property, and the deadliness of the sin which perverts it from its usefulness by avarice or waste.

Gluttony, the sixth mortal sin, is of a more private nature than avarice. Avarice touches at once the material bond of the practical will-power of society, while gluttony, or intemperance, only unfits the individual to fulfill his functions as a member of institutions, — the family, civil society, the state, or the church. By this sin the good that would flow from him is greatly diminished, or entirely cut off. He sinks down below the condition of the brute, and follows appetite alone, thus paralyzing his will, and cutting himself off from the rulership over nature in time and space.

Lust attacks the institution of the family. It is a deadly sin, because the family is the element of all other institutions: it is their material presupposition. It is placed above intemperance as less harmful, because the latter is nearly as destructive to the family, and much more destructive to the industrial well-being of society, and because intemperance leads more directly to the sins of sloth and anger or violence.

With this survey of the scope of sin, let us turn back for a moment to the great question of the origin of the consciousness of sin. Inasmuch as the consciousness of the freedom of the will has not existed throughout human history, so the consciousness of sin has not always existed in the sense in which Christian nations possess it. With those Oriental peoples that profess the religions of Brahmanism or Buddhism, there is no such thing possible as a consciousness of sin as such. They hold that all things finite are evil, and, moreover, that all things are illusionary or dream-existences. It is not a purified will that one desires, but the utter annihilation of all will. The first Nidâna of the Buddhists is ignorance (of this fact that all existing things are a dream). The second Nidâna is action. For if we really believe that the world exists, we next set about acting upon it in order to change it.

As Brahma is pure being, he is neither good nor evil. And no human action can be essentially good or evil. Hence there can be no sin in our sense of the word.

The Hebrew consciousness is the first to conceive the idea of sin, and it is very important to notice that the idea arises only when a God is conceived as something purely spiritual and apart from nature. Jehovah is not the spirit of the earth, or ocean, or the sky, or the thunderstorm, or of any other natural power. All these are to him mere instruments, or even mere playthings. He does not care for sacred places, but only for the recognition of human beings. Nor does he care for mere abstract ceremonial worship. Righteousness and goodness are his own attributes, and he loves only men who resemble him in these qualities.

Here we see the concept of sin arise. There is an ideal in each man of righteousness and goodness, the ideal which he conceives of Jehovah, and which Jehovah has revealed to his people. Measured by the standard of this ideal, the individual finds himself stained by nature. He sees his distance from the separately subsisting substance of Jehovah, a pure spirit, and recognizes not only his fallen condition, but also his constant imperfection in willing the just and good.

Righteousness and goodness signify justice and mercy. Justice holds the individual responsible for his deeds, whatever they are; if they are injurious towards others, they shall be turned back upon him to punish him. He shall reap the result of his own deeds.

Goodness means mercy, and in this attribute Jehovah is long-suffering towards human creatures, and forgives their shortcomings. In the new dispensation, which is Christianity, God is represented as self-sacrificing for the benefit of his imperfect creatures. He condescends from on High to take up human life, and to die for the salvation of men.

Only in a religion which recognizes God's image in man can this idea of sin arise. Only as measured against that lofty ideal of divine humanity can the individual feel the utter inadequacy of his own doings and endeavors.

Next we must note especially that sin is more and more concretely defined by the Christian consciousness. The words of Christ, " Inasmuch as ye do it unto the least of these ye do it unto me," have continually prompted to the exercise of the missionary spirit, and it is strictly true that the third Person of the Trinity is an institutional Personality. He is the spirit of the Invisible Church, the new Jerusalem, the City of God. The word "City" calls up at once the social element of human nature in its highest realization of mutual helpfulness.

In the light of this idea of the Holy Spirit, which fills all members of the Invisible Church, and makes all participant in the fullness of the divine life, we see the principle that guided Dante in his portrayal of the effects of sin. Sin is everywhere with him the antagonism of the free will against the special institutions which are functions of the one great institution, the Invisible Church. Antagonism to the Holy Spirit is the essence of all sin.

It is true that Dante found the great outlines of his doctrine in the ethical systems of his time, derived as they were from the structure of Aristotle's ethics. But Dante has not copied anything without making it over, and adding new and important features.

While the seven mortal sins come in their proper shape in the Purgatorio, there are some of them so modified in the Inferno as to be not easily recognized.

Instead of Pride and Envy and Anger and Sloth, we have the daughters of Pride, the daughters of Envy, and the daughters of Anger and Sloth, — as the effects of these sins are called by the Scholastic theologians. The daughters of Pride are four s... reachery. The daughters of Envy are ... s... of fraud. Sloth has sullenness and lukewarmness, and perhaps disbelief in immortality, as its daughters.

But more important than anything else in Dante's conception of sin is his discrimination of the immediate effects of sin in producing the Inferno from the mediating effects in producing the Purgatorio.

The immediate effect of sin is to cause an internal separation of the sinner from the social whole in which he lives. His sin forms for him an atmosphere of the Inferno. There is a sort of honest belief on the part of the sinner in the Inferno that his cause is a just one. He believes in individualism, and thinks that his pain is inflicted upon him from outside. Dante hears a great din when he enters the first round of the Inferno proper; in this din he distinguishes the voices of cursing, — God, parents, neighbors, mankind, all are cursed, the total environment, all but the sinner's own self is cursed.

To be in the Inferno one must have this implicit

belief in one's self as the true centre of the universe. If one sees that the social whole, the institutions of civilization, are one's deeper self, and that God is the true self, then all the punishment of the Inferno becomes purgatorial, and leads towards a renunciation of sin as unprofitable.

But the Purgatory proper has a quite different atmosphere. The tendency to sin is not overcome, but the knowledge is reached that sin is negative to the true self. The soul in Purgatory, therefore, desires above all to be rid of the tendency to sin. Hence he rejoices in the pain. The ministration of pain as God's angel has become manifest. God holds down his hand to lift up the sinner, and this hand is pain. Hence the souls in the Purgatorio desire to endure all of the purifying tortures that meet them. In the round of anger they breathe the thick smoke, and in the round of lust they keep within the chastening flames.

To the soul who has learned so much of the freedom of the will as permits him to see that all influences from the environment, all the arrows of fate, all the stings of fortune, may be made use of by the soul to purify itself, to such a soul no evil can happen. He has solved the problem of life.

The purgatorial attitude towards pain is this one of resignation and purification. To the proud in the lowest round of the Inferno, the environment of the soul is a solid mass of ice. Human society has become chilled and frozen so far as they are concerned. They have treated their fellow-men with utter contempt until a reaction has set in which shuts them out from all participation in the common good. They are frozen out by society because they have by their own actions rendered social intercourse impossible. The ice in which they are immersed is the reaction of their own deeds.

Man's ideal spiritual state is one of participation with his fellow-men. He does something for them, and they do something for him. He pursues some special vocation, and gaining great skill by limiting himself to one kind of work, he is able to produce much more than he would do were he to undertake all things. But this division of labor renders necessary a complete system of interdependence. Each one depends upon the rest for what he does not produce himself; that is to say, for all articles of food, clothing, and shelter, except the limited item that he produces.

But this process of division of labor, and limitation of work to narrow specialties, so increases skill that the total product of all society is multiplied a hundred-fold, and the share of each is thus increased to that extent. Hence, in the matter of food, clothing, and shelter, and the comforts of life, social union means emancipation from drudgery and the pinchings of want.

But with the mutual interchange of material productions in social union, there goes on the far more important interchange of intellectual and moral experience. Each person has something unique in his own experience, something that he has seen or felt that no one else has. And yet all the feelings and thoughts, all the life-experiences of each individual, are possibilities of all other individuals. The total revelation of humanity — humanity in all its possibilities — can only be made through the entire race. Each individual's life-experience is only a fragment of this revelation of human nature. How infinitely important it is, therefore, that each person shall behold the spectacle of this revelation of humanity in others. What lies in him potentially, and what would take millions of years to realize, he may see all realized in his fellow-men around him.

Thus what is impossible becomes possible. A man enjoys the fruits of experience vicariously. He lives through the lives of others. All that they have seen is treasured and reported to him, all that they have reflected is also given to him. The collisions which they have made against the moral law, the collisions against the state, the family, and the church, all these collisions and their results on themselves, and on society, are described and communicated one to another, and by low aggregations make up the experience of the race. And this experience is the inheritance of all who receive the training and culture of civilization.

The truly precious advantages that the individual gains from society are therefore not so much his share in the productive industry of the world — his food, clothing, and shelter — as this spiritual gift of the experience of the race made for him vicariously. For all human life is, as we have seen, vicarious, each one living for all others, and rendering unnecessary the pain and inconvenience incidental to making the experiments in one's own person.

Sin is, as we have explained, an attack on the institutions which make possible this vicarious experience. A deadly sin, if persisted in, would cut off the individual from its benefits, and if all persons practiced this sin, society would become impossible.

Here we come again to the definition of the Inferno. The state of mind in which a person commits a deadly sin is a state of alienation as regards giving and receiving, — one or both.

For to participate in the benefits of society one must both give and receive, must give one's individual contributions to the wisdom of the race, and in return receive with humility and faith the aggregate wisdom stored up in all places and all ages.

As soon as one assumes the frame of mind in which he may will to commit a deadly sin, he places himself in the Inferno.

Dante's genius enables him to poetically describe these states of mind that are inseparably connected with the feelings and conviction which lead to the commission of those sins. The lustful are driven about by whirlwinds of passion under a dark and gloomy sky; the intemperate suffer internally and externally such foul diseases as we see in Dante's symbols. The avaricious and prodigal heave heavy weights; that is to say, they are seen lifting and carrying the pelf for its own sake, instead of making their wealth carry and serve them. The angry are plunged beneath putrid mud; for anger is a muddy and smoky state of the soul, wherein one can neither give nor receive spiritual truth. The hypocrites are seen to wear heavy leaden cloaks gilded outside, — heavy cloaks of make-believe. Those who give and take bribes are plunged in boiling pitch, for they cannot escape from the blackmail that is to be levied upon them, — their evil companions sticking to them like pitch. The evil counselors are immersed in tongues of living flame, for their tongues produce this flame of discord.

The fortune-tellers and those who believe them are looking on the future as though it were a fixed event, — as if it were, in fact, all past, — and hence their necks are twisted round so that their faces gaze on the way that they have come, and not before them on the way that they are still to go. For to the soothsayer all is, in fact, turned into the past. Symbolically his neck is so twisted that his face looks backward as he walks forward into the future.

Thieves change shapes with serpents; the thief does not retain even his own person, because he makes all property insecure. Again, the thief is assuming disguises, and inwardly changing himself into the serpent that secretly and noiselessly glides upon its prey.

Such as these are the poetic devices of Dante to indicate the state of mind of sinners in the Inferno.

In the Purgatorio, on the other hand, we have the state of mind of repentant sinners who see the true relation of their deeds to their own best interests. There the proud see themselves as laboring to support enormous weights that bend them double, and almost crush them to the earth. For the proud man wishes to be all in all without the help of society. He wishes to bear the weight of the entire universe alone on his shoulders. Hence Dante symbolizes this true view of the relation of the sinner to his pride. To the repentant sinner envy is seen to be a sort of iron thread that sews up one's eyes and does not permit him to see the good of his fellow-men. Dante shows us, too, how the repenting sinner sees anger to be a thick, suffocating smoke.

When one finds the steep slope of Purgatory as easy to climb as it is to glide down the river in a boat, then he has reached the top of the mount, and may now enter the Paradiso.

The spirit of the Purgatorio is, as we have shown, that of a mind that rejoices more in the pain that comes as a schoolmaster after the sin, than it does in the sinful objects gained. The spirit of the Inferno is bitter and revengeful, every man's hand raised against everybody else. The spirit of the Purgatorio is that of meek submission to the pain encountered from without, using all opportunity for purification through the ministration of pain.

The spirit of the Paradiso is positive. It is not like Purgatory, the elimination of selfishness, but it is the joyful participation with all human brothers in doing the good and knowing the true.

Thus Dante sees the nature of sin to be a self-obscuration of the soul, curable by means of repentance and the assertion of the free will that assumes the form of willing the divine will and renouncing the selfish will.

Freedom makes sin and freedom renounces sin. Sin is its own punishment. Since sin arises through freedom, the freedom to repent always remains to the sinner, both here and hereafter.

There can be no cessation of hell except as a consequence of the cessation of sin and the turning to repentance.

Freedom always belongs to separate substances, as Dante and the Scholastics denominate men, angels and God. Hence the punishments of the Inferno, so long as they exist, demonstrate the freedom of the sinner, and prove that he is still in probation. He may at any moment enter Purgatory, and then all his pain becomes remedial and purifying.

www.ingramcontent.com/pod-product-compliance
Lightning Source LLC
Chambersburg PA
CBHW020827230426
43666CB00007B/1125